Biography Today

Profiles of People of Interest to Young Readers

Scientists & Inventors

Volume 9

Cherie D. Abbey
Managing Editor

Kevin Hillstrom
Editor

615 Griswold Street • Detroit, Michigan 48226

Cherie D. Abbey, *Managing Editor*
Kevin Hillstrom, *Editor*
Jeff Hill, Laurie Hillstrom, Sara Pendergast, Tom Pendergast, Diane Telgen,
Sue Ellen Thompson, Matt Totsky, Rhoda Wilburn, *Staff Writers*
Barry Puckett, *Research Associate*
Allison A. Beckett, Mary Butler, and Linda Strand, *Research Assistants*

Omnigraphics, Inc.

* * *

Matthew P. Barbour, *Senior Vice President*
Kay Gill, *Vice President — Directories*
Kevin Hayes, *Operations Manager*
Leif Gruenberg, *Development Manager*
David P. Bianco, *Marketing Director*

* * *

Peter E. Ruffner, *Publisher*
Frederick G. Ruffner, Jr., *Chairman*

The information in this publication was compiled from the sources cited and from other sources considered reliable. While every possible effort has been made to ensure reliability, the publisher will not assume liability for damages caused by inaccuracies in the data, and makes no warranty, express or implied, on the accuracy of the information contained herein.

This book is printed on acid-free paper meeting the ANSI Z39.48 Standard. The infinity symbol that appears above indicates that the paper in this book meets that standard.

Printed in the United States

Contents

Preface

Welcome to the ninth volume of the **Biography Today Scientists and Inventors** Series. We are publishing this series in response to suggestions from our readers, who want more coverage of more people in *Biography Today*. Several volumes, covering **Artists, Authors, Performing Artists, Scientists and Inventors, Sports Figures, and World Leaders,** have appeared thus far in the Subject Series. Each of these hardcover volumes is 200 pages in length and covers approximately 10 individuals of interest to readers ages 9 and above. The length and format of the entries are like those found in the regular issues of *Biography Today*, but there is **no duplication** between the regular series and the special subject volumes.

The Plan of the Work

As with the regular issues of *Biography Today*, this special subject volume on **Scientists and Inventors** was especially created to appeal to young readers in a format they can enjoy reading and readily understand. Each volume contains alphabetically arranged sketches. Each entry provides at least one picture of the individual profiled, and bold-faced rubrics lead the reader to information on birth, youth, early memories, education, first jobs, marriage and family, career highlights, memorable experiences, hobbies, and honors and awards. Each of the entries ends with a list of easily accessible sources designed to lead the student to further reading on the individual and a current address. Obituary entries are also included, written to provide a perspective on the individual's entire career. Obituaries are clearly marked in both the table of contents and at the beginning of the entry.

Biographies are prepared by Omnigraphics editors after extensive research, utilizing the most current materials available. Those sources that are generally available to students appear in the list of further reading at the end of the sketch.

Indexes

A new index now appears in all *Biography Today* publications. In an effort to make the index easier to use, we have combined the **Name** and **General Index** into one, called the **Cumulative Index**. This new index contains the names of all individuals who have appeared in *Biography Today* since the series began. The names appear in bold faced type, followed by the issue in which they appeared. The Cumulative Index also contains the occupations, nationalities, and ethnic and minority origins of individuals profiled. The Cumulative Index is cumulative, including references to all individuals who have appeared in the *Biography Today* General Series and the *Biography Today* Special Subject volumes since the series began in 1992.

The Birthday Index and Places of Birth Index will continue to appear in all Special Subject volumes.

Our Advisors

This series was reviewed by an Advisory Board comprised of librarians, children's literature specialists, and reading instructors to ensure that the concept of this publication — to provide a readable and accessible biographical magazine for young readers — was on target. They evaluated the title as it developed, and their suggestions have proved invaluable. Any errors, however, are ours alone. We'd like to list the Advisory Board members, and to thank them for their efforts.

Sandra Arden, *Retired*
Assistant Director
Troy Public Library, Troy, MI

Gail Beaver
University of Michigan School of Information
Ann Arbor, MI

Marilyn Bethel, *Retired*
Broward County Public Library System
Fort Lauderdale, FL

Nancy Bryant
Brookside School Library,
Cranbrook Educational Community
Bloomfield Hills, MI

Cindy Cares
Southfield Public Library
Southfield, MI

Linda Carpino
Detroit Public Library
Detroit, MI

Carol Doll
Wayne State University Library and Information Science Program
Detroit, MI

Helen Gregory
Grosse Pointe Public Library
Grosse Pointe, MI

Jane Klasing, *Retired*
School Board of Broward County
Fort Lauderdale, FL

Marlene Lee
Broward County Public Library System
Fort Lauderdale, FL

Sylvia Mavrogenes
Miami-Dade Public Library System
Miami, FL

Carole J. McCollough
Detroit, MI

Rosemary Orlando
St. Clair Shores Public Library
St. Clair Shores, MI

Renee Schwartz
Broward County Public Library System
Fort Lauderdale, FL

Lee Sprince
Broward West Regional Library
Fort Lauderdale, FL

Susan Stewart, *Retired*
Birney Middle School Reading Laboratory, Southfield, MI

Ethel Stoloff, *Retired*
Birney Middle School Library
Southfield, MI

Our Advisory Board stressed to us that we should not shy away from controversial or unconventional people in our profiles, and we have tried to follow their advice. The Advisory Board also mentioned that the sketches might be useful in reluctant reader and adult literacy programs, and we would value any comments librarians might have about the suitability of our magazine for those purposes.

Your Comments Are Welcome

Our goal is to be accurate and up-to-date, to give young readers information they can learn from and enjoy. Now we want to know what you think. Take a look at this issue of *Biography Today*, on approval. Write or call me with your comments. We want to provide an excellent source of biographical information for young people. Let us know how you think we're doing.

Cherie Abbey
Managing Editor, *Biography Today*
Omnigraphics, Inc.
615 Griswold Street
Detroit, MI 48226

editor@biographytoday.com
www.biographytoday.com

Robert Barron 1942?-

American Anaplastologist (Prosthetic Designer and Sculptor)
Former CIA Disguise Artist and Founder of Custom Prosthetic Designs, Inc.

BIRTH

Robert Barron was born around 1942 in DuQuoin, Illinois. His parents, Bette and Phil Barron, owned a clothing store in DuQuoin. Robert is the oldest of their three children. He has one sister, Barbara Conte. Barron also had a brother, Donald, who died in 1986.

YOUTH

Barron enjoyed growing up in DuQuoin, a small coal-mining town in southern Illinois, near St. Louis, Missouri. "It was fun growing up in a quaint place like DuQuoin," he recalled. "We had close family ties. It's a town where everybody knows each other and they pitch in helping each other. It's kind of nice."

Even as a young child, Barron liked things to be neat and orderly. He always carefully arranged his toys and clothes in his room. Barron's mother recalled that when he was five years old, he would even "paint" his swing set with water "to make it look brand new." He also spent many hours coloring, always being mindful of staying within the lines. Before long, he could draw with either hand. As he grew older, his interest in art and drawing remained strong. "My original [career] goal was to work for Hallmark cards," Barron remembered.

By the time he reached high school, Barron had developed a particular fascination with art that created the illusion of reality. One year, he spent five months working on a landscape painting of the Grand Canyon, paying special attention to the picture's lighting and depth. He subsequently entered the painting in an art contest at the annual state fair. When he looked for his artwork at the fair, he initially could not find it among the other paintings. He eventually discovered that the fair organizers had mistaken his painting for a photograph and entered it into the photography contest. The judges were fooled as well, for they awarded Barron a blue ribbon for the painting in the photography category.

EDUCATION

Barron attended elementary and high school in DuQuoin. One of his favorite high school instructors was his art teacher, Irene Brock, who encouraged him to develop his artistic talents. After earning his diploma, he spent two years at nearby Southern Illinois University — Carbondale. His mentor at Carbondale was Professor Dan Bozz, who taught in the commercial art department. Barron graduated in 1962 with a degree in commercial art.

CAREER HIGHLIGHTS

Instead of pursuing a career in art after graduating from college, Barron returned to his hometown to help his parents in their store. In 1965 Barron joined the United States Marine Corps, as the U.S. was becoming involved in the Vietnam War. Like many other young American men of that era, he believed that if he enlisted instead of waiting for a possible draft notice, he would be less likely to see combat in Vietnam. Aware of Barron's artistic talents, the Marines assigned him to design graphic training aids at a base in Okinawa, Japan. He served in the Marines for four years, attaining the rank of sergeant. In his last months of military service, he helped design exhibits at the Navy and Marine Corps Exhibit Center in Washington, D.C.

In 1968 Barron left the Marines to take a job at the Pentagon, the headquarters of the U.S. military in Arlington, Virginia. He started in the Office of the Chief of Naval Operations as an illustrator and then moved up to art director for *Directions*, the Navy's public affairs quarterly magazine. Barron enjoyed his work, but he disliked the amount of time he spent commuting to work and hunting down a parking spot. He eventually decided to make his own parking permit so that he could park in the spaces reserved for the Pentagon's top officials. "I didn't like the 15-minute walk to the Pentagon," he explained. "I went out and 'borrowed' a parking permit from one of the unlocked cars. I took down all the proper dimensions, colors, and notations—all the things you need to forge a document." Barron used this permit for about a year, until one of his co-workers turned him in. The punishment for this felony could have been as much as $2,000, but the traffic court judge fined him only $50. According to Barron, the judge jokingly told him, "Now I know where I can get a parking permit."

"I started working in the graphics arts division [of the CIA], which specialized in the forgery of documents," recalled Barron. "I became one of their main forgers and eventually became a disguise specialist."

Embarking on a Career in the CIA

Two weeks after his court appearance, Barron was contacted by a man who said he worked for another government agency and wanted to talk to him about his artistic skills. A short time later, he met two men in a nondescript office for the first of a series of interviews, tests, and physical and polygraph (lie detector) exams.

The mysterious man's employer turned out to be the Central Intelligence Agency (CIA), the chief intelligence-gathering agency of the U.S. government. Barron eventually learned that the traffic judge who had fined him

11

had been so impressed by his forgery skills that he passed Barron's name on to a friend who worked in the CIA. After two months of extensive interviews, Barron accepted a position with the CIA.

Barron spent his first year at the CIA learning his way around. "I started working in the graphics arts division, which specialized in the forgery of documents," he said. He gradually became an expert at forging everything from passports to "pocket litter" (movie ticket stubs, receipts, worn address books) for agents to carry around in the field. "I became one of their main forgers and eventually became a disguise specialist," Barron related.

In the early 1970s the CIA sent Barron to eastern Asia, where he created disguises for undercover agents. Armed with Barron's disguises, some Caucasian case officers were able to pass for ethnic Asians. In addition to the disguises, Barron forged identity papers, passports, and pocket litter for the agents to carry with them.

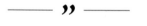

"If you had a disguise that didn't look right or drew attention, then you were in trouble. It could cost you your life."

In 1974 Barron returned to Washington, D.C., to work as a full-time disguise specialist. The CIA sent him to Hollywood to soak up knowledge from some of the movie industry's leading make-up artists. For example, he briefly trained with John Chambers, a special-effects expert known for creating the ape suits that were used in the 1968 version of the *Planet of the Apes* movie. Although Barron picked up some ideas from these make-up artists, he understood that cameras and touch-up editing were capable of hiding some of the imperfections of the "disguises" in the movies. In the real world, however, field agents cannot count on such factors to hide imperfections in their disguises. Their disguises must be convincing in broad daylight from as close as 12 inches away. According to Barron, "If you had a disguise that didn't look right or drew attention, then you were in trouble. It could cost you your life."

Keenly aware of the stakes involved, Barron took his work very seriously. His dedication enabled him to disguise countless agents so that they could survive in what retired CIA deputy director Herb Saunders called "the murky world of the intelligence trade." By the early 1980s, Barron had created disguises for agents all around the world, including those stationed in Russia, China, Ethiopia, Bulgaria, Germany, Czechoslovakia, Somalia, Kuwait, Japan, and various South American nations. But while Barron took

Barron has used his artistic talents to create a wide range of prosthetics for accident victims and people suffering from birth defects.

his work very seriously, he also displayed a sense of humor. He regularly used his talents to play practical jokes on fellow staff members. On one occasion he wore a disguise to an event attended by former U.S. Attorney General Janet Reno. When he finally met Reno, he startled the former attorney general by ripping off his mask right in front of her.

Growing Fascination with Prosthetics

Over time, Barron developed his own sophisticated airbrush painting techniques in creating disguises. But he was always looking for new disguise techniques, and in the early 1980s he began to investigate prosthetics (artificial limbs and other body parts) as a possible tool. He was particularly inspired by a 1983 visit to a symposium of the Association of Biomedical

Sculptors. Many of the lecturers showed how prosthetics were being used to help people who suffered disfigurement caused by disease, injury, or birth defects. As Barron listened to these presentations, he began to think that if he applied his skills to prosthetics, he could make life easier for many people. "I knew then, when I saw these poor people and the torment and humiliation they had to go through because of their disfigurement, that it would be really nice to help heal them," he said.

Barron continued to work on disguises for the CIA for the next ten years. During that time, however, he also received instruction from Professor Dennis Lee, who was the head of the University of Michigan Medical Sculpture Unit. Barron proved to be an exceptionally gifted student. "There are only 20 good [medical sculptors] in the country, and Bob is as good as I've seen," declared Lee. "His colorations are incredible. He's a tremendous artist and sculptor."

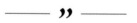

"My job was putting people in hiding, and now my job is bringing people out of hiding," Barron said.

Barron retired from the CIA in 1993. In recognition of his 24 years of service to the agency, he was awarded the Career Intelligence Medal. "His artistic skills were unmatched," wrote former CIA director James Woolsey. "He was the impetus of the advanced disguise system and the ideal by which all other disguise officers are judged."

Taking on New Challenges

After Barron retired from the CIA, he started his own company, Custom Prosthetic Designs, Inc. Working as an anaplastologist, a prosthetic designer and sculptor, he began producing prosthetic ears, eyes, noses, hands, and masks for people suffering from disfigurement. "My job was putting people in hiding, and now my job is bringing people out of hiding," Barron declared.

Barron's first patient was a middle-aged man who had lost an eye and most of the surrounding cheek and nasal passages to cancer. Surgical reconstruction was not an option in his case, but Barron created an orbital eye prosthetic that was so life-like that the patient cried with happiness upon viewing himself in the mirror. "I'll remember that expression as long as I live," said Barron. His later patients ranged in age from very young children to elderly adults. For example, he created an ear for an eight-year-old girl born with most of one ear missing. He also constructed a new eye for a 75-year-old retired travel agent who had lost one of her eyes to cancer. "There's no better feeling than to help someone who's been dealt a difficult hand, to give them hope, to make their day go a little easier," he said.

Over the course of several years, Barron also developed close working relationships with other specialists, including Craig Dufresne, a reconstructive plastic surgeon, and Michael T. Singer and Jeffery Lane, both of whom are dentists. All of these professionals are proud of their association with Barron. "Bob [Barron] fills an important and long-empty niche," declared Dufresne. "He makes it possible to join medicine and art, surgery and sculpture."

In most cases, Barron's work follows the same general steps. Using various clays, plasters, and chemicals, Barron takes an impression of the damaged area and uses it to make a plaster mold. He fills the mold with a layer of acrylic resin to cast the area. He then repeats the process with a healthy substitute. For example, if he is working on creating a prosthetic ear, he will copy the patient's good ear and make a mirror image of it. Because Barron is a perfectionist, it sometimes takes him several tries before he will even attempt to fit a prosthetic on a patient. But it is precisely his perfectionist attitude that enables him to make such life-like prosthetics. When Barron fits the prosthetic on the patient, he must trim and adjust the device. He also tints it to match the patient's skin tones. He even adds such features as veins, hair, blemishes, freckles, wrinkles, and moles to make the appearance more realistic. "Each prosthetic device is unique and takes its own amount of time," stated Barron. "It never gets easier because each piece demands inspiration and creativity."

> **"There's no better feeling than to help someone who's been dealt a difficult hand, to give them hope, to make their day go a little easier."**

Barron notes that many of his prosthetic devices serve a medical as well as a cosmetic purpose. For example, a well-made prosthetic nose can help keep the mucous membranes from drying out and improve a patient's speech. Prosthetic ears can improve the patient's hearing as much as 20 percent by collecting sound waves and drawing them into the auditory canals. They can also keep foreign elements out and allow a patient to wear glasses.

As his second career blossomed, Barron continued to use his talents to help people whose lives had been turned upside down by violence or disaster. For example, he donated his time to a surgical team that created new eyes, ears, and a nose for a pregnant Pakistani mother of four whose husband had repeatedly slashed her face in a jealous rage. He also is proud of the full-face prosthetic he created for a man who had been trapped in a burning car for 20 minutes. By the time he was rescued, the victim's face had been so badly burned that he could not bear to have people look at him. He retreated to his home and became a recluse. Barron, however, was able to reconstruct the man's entire face and hair from old photographs. The mask he created is suspended above the patient's fragile skin grafts. Although the patient still cannot move the mouth of the mask, he is no longer afraid to go out in public when he wears the mask. Barron also created a second mask for the patient that covers only the upper portion of his face so that he can use his mouth to eat and drink.

> *"There's a purpose in life," said Barron. "When I was young and death defying in the [CIA], I didn't think of my work that way — till people would say, 'Thanks for saving my life.' Now I'm conscious of my purpose."*

Seeing God's Hand in His Work

Barron ran his company from the basement of his home for ten years. In the spring of 2003, he moved into an office suite in Ashburn, Virginia. Although the office looks and feels like a medical doctor's office and Barron refers to his clients as "patients," Barron is quick to point out that he is not a doctor. Whatever his medical credentials, though, he has helped hundreds of people build better lives for themselves. "My purpose is to help people," Barron stated. "The good Lord gave me a gift, and I know he's using me to help others."

Indeed, Barron believes that he is doing God's work. According to Barron, he has been in several life-threatening incidents over the years, including a serious car accident; a gas furnace explosion that caused him to suffer three months of blindness; an incident in which he almost drowned; and a bout with cancer. But each time, he has picked himself up and resumed his life. "I guess the good Lord saved me all along so He could use me to help others," Barron said. "There's a purpose in life. When I was young and death defying in the [CIA], I didn't think of my work that way — till people would say, 'Thanks for saving my life.' Now I'm conscious of my purpose. Deep down, I'm still wild and mostly out of control. But this work keeps me under control."

Today, Barron is one of approximately 75 people in the United States engaged in the sort of prosthetic work that he does. But few of his colleagues are as well known. Barron has made guest appearances on "The Oprah Winfrey Show," ABC's "Prime Time Thursday" news show, and the Discovery Channel. He has also been featured in *Reader's Digest* and *People* magazines.

MARRIAGE AND FAMILY

Robert Barron is twice divorced. He was most recently married to Carol Barron. He has two grown sons, Mark and Todd.

HOBBIES AND OTHER INTERESTS

Barron's passion for his work leaves him little time for recreational pursuits. It is not unusual for him to work seven days a week, arriving at work at 7:00 a.m. and staying until 11:00 p.m. or later. "I'll continue to do this job as long as I can I see, as long as my hands are steady," he stated. "Everyone has a purpose in life. And I have found my purpose." Barron does make time to attend church every Sunday, and he occasionally takes his boat out for an afternoon on the water.

FURTHER READING

Periodicals

Arizona Republic, July 7, 2002, p.A1
Fredericksburg (VA) Free-Lance Star, Aug. 5, 2002
People, Feb. 11, 2002, p.111
Readers Digest, Mar. 2001, p.128
Southern Illinoisan, Mar. 27, 2002
Washington Post, Jan. 12, 2003, p.F1
Washington Times, June 2, 1994, p. C10; June 6, 2003, p.C8
Washingtonian, June 2000, p.112

Additional information for this profile was gathered from "The Oprah Winfrey Show," broadcast July 23, 2003.

Online Articles

http://www.abcnews.com
 (*ABCNews.com,* "A New Face: Prosthetics Designer Helps Disfigured People Return to the Public Life," Mar. 20, 2002)

ADDRESS

Robert R. Barron
Custom Prosthetic Designs, Inc.
20608 Gordon Park Square, Suite 150
Ashburn, VA 20147

WORLD WIDE WEB SITE

http://www.prosthesis.com

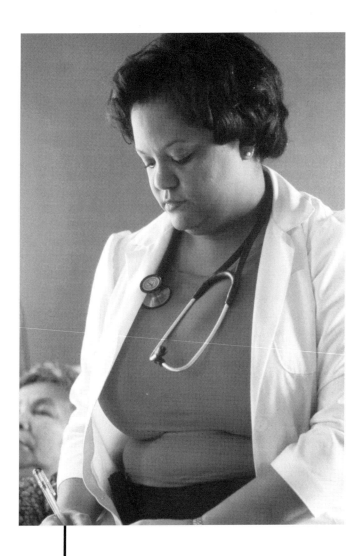

Regina Benjamin 1956-
American Physician and Health Care Activist
Founder of the Bayou LaBatre Rural Health Clinic

BIRTH

Regina Benjamin was born in 1956 in Mobile, Alabama. She was the second of two children born to Clarence Benjamin, a civil servant, and his wife Millie. Her older brother, Clarence, died in 1996.

YOUTH

Benjamin grew up on Alabama's Gulf Coast in Daphne, a suburb of Mobile. Her parents divorced when she was very young. She and her brother were raised by their mother, who worked long hours as a waitress to support them. Benjamin grew up in what most people would consider poverty, yet she never thought of her family as poor. "I didn't know I was poor until someone in junior high school told me I was," she recalled. "I grew up fishing and crabbing [in the waters of the Gulf of Mexico], so we always had plenty of good food."

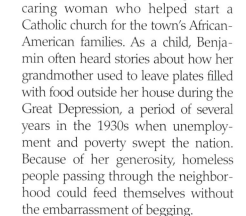

> "[My mother] was very intelligent, very bright, witty and extremely social and outgoing, very much a team and consensus builder, and very opinionated," recalled Benjamin. "Many of those traits I inherited from my mother."

One of the biggest influences in Benjamin's early development was her maternal grandmother, an energetic and caring woman who helped start a Catholic church for the town's African-American families. As a child, Benjamin often heard stories about how her grandmother used to leave plates filled with food outside her house during the Great Depression, a period of several years in the 1930s when unemployment and poverty swept the nation. Because of her generosity, homeless people passing through the neighborhood could feed themselves without the embarrassment of begging.

The other major influence in Benjamin's life was her mother. Millie Benjamin made it clear that she expected her daughter to do something special with her life. Although she didn't steer her specifically toward a career in medicine, she urged Regina to take advantage of the opportunities available to her and to push for excellence in everything she did. "She kept my grandmother's values alive in us," Regina Benjamin recalled. "She was very intelligent, very bright, witty and extremely social and outgoing, very much a team and consensus builder, and very opinionated. Many of those traits I inherited from my mother. It wasn't until after my mother died that I realized the influence she had on me."

EDUCATION

Benjamin received her elementary and high school education in the Mobile area. As she approached graduation from Fairhope High School in

Fairhope, Alabama, Benjamin thought about pursing a career in international law. After earning her high school diploma in 1975, she enrolled at Xavier University in New Orleans, Louisiana. Shortly after her arrival, however, she met an African-American doctor. "I had never seen a black doctor before," she recalled. This meeting inspired her to change her career plans and pursue a medical career.

After earning a bachelor of science degree in chemistry in 1979, Benjamin knew that she could not afford to continue her education without securing some sort of financial assistance. She decided to sign up for the National Health Service Corps (NHSC), a government program that covers medical school tuition for students. In return, participants in the program agree to donate their skills to needy communities for three years after graduation. After enrolling in the NHSC, Benjamin spent two years at the Morehouse School of Medicine in Atlanta. She then moved on to the University of Alabama Medical School in Birmingham. She earned a master's degree in medicine in 1984, specializing in family practice. She then completed two years of family-practice residency training in Macon, Georgia.

Benjamin also took business classes after opening her practice. She earned a master's degree in business administration from Tulane University in New Orleans in 1991.

CAREER HIGHLIGHTS

Benjamin's involvement with the National Health Service Corps proved to be a life-changing experience for her. After completing her residency training in Georgia in 1987, she was delighted to hear that the NHSC had decided to place her in her home state of Alabama. She was assigned to the Mostellar Medical Center in Irvington, Alabama, where she spent the next three years helping tend to the medical needs of the townspeople. She found this work so rewarding that—after fulfilling her commitment to the NHSC—she decided to open her own clinic. "Throughout my life, nothing has ever been planned," she said. "I am a firm believer that you bloom wherever you're planted."

Benjamin decided to open her clinic in nearby Bayou LaBatre, a small town of about 2,500 people on Alabama's Gulf Coast that is best known as the setting for the 1994 film *Forrest Gump.* Most of the town's residents make their living in the shrimp industry, and the vast majority live below the poverty line. "This is a community where folks are too poor to afford medical care, but too rich to qualify for Medicaid [a government program that helps impoverished people pay for medical expenses]," she explained. "I like the people and I can make a difference here."

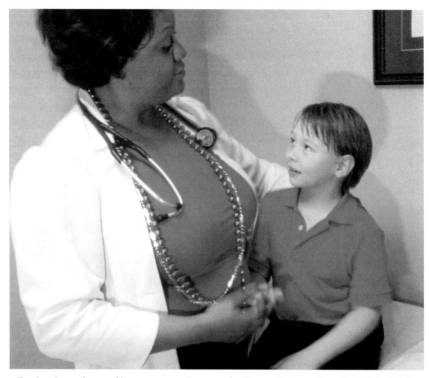

Benjamin and one of her young patients at the Bayou LaBatre Rural Health Clinic.

Benjamin opened her practice in Bayou LaBatre in 1990. Within a matter of months, she became one of the community's most trusted and respected members. She treated a variety of injuries and illnesses, many of which were linked to fishing in the Gulf. Cases of "shrimp poisoning," a skin condition that comes from handling shrimp, were common, as were cuts, shark bites, and even frostbite from the giant freezers that were used in the town's seafood plants. When it became clear that many of her patients could not afford to pay for their treatment, Benjamin let them pay her five or ten dollars a week. She accepted other forms of payment as well, ranging from buckets of fresh-caught shrimp or oysters to homemade pies and handpicked pecans. Before long, her office was decorated with arts and crafts created by grateful townspeople. "If they're sick, they've got to be treated, and then you worry about the bill later," Benjamin explained. "You can't get money from somebody who doesn't have it."

As the months passed, Benjamin helped her patients in other ways as well. She helped many patients deal with insurance problems, arguing with insurance companies on their behalf for hours at a time. She also arranged transportation for elderly patients without access to cars, and she regularly visited people who were housebound by their illnesses.

Since the clinic did not bring in enough money for Benjamin to pay herself a salary, she worked weekends as an emergency room doctor at hospitals and nursing homes an hour or more away. This extra work enabled her to meet her personal living expenses and hire a small nursing staff for the clinic. Still, she recognized that she needed to run her practice more efficiently. With this in mind, she enrolled in the MBA (master of business administration) program at Tulane. For the next 18 months she commuted 125 miles to school on weekends to study finance and accounting. At the same time, she continued to meet all the medical needs of her patients in Bayou LaBatre.

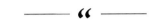

During her studies at Tulane, Benjamin discovered that federal financial aid could be requested for health facilities in rural areas like Bayou LaBatre. Armed with this knowledge, she closed her private practice and opened a rural health clinic. The federal grants and donations she secured enabled her to stop moonlighting as an emergency room doctor. In 2002

"If they're sick, they've got to be treated, and then you worry about the bill later," Benjamin said. "You can't get money from somebody who doesn't have it."

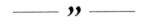

Benjamin gained nonprofit status for the clinic, making it eligible for additional state and federal grants. "I want the clinic to be able to survive without me if I die in a plane crash tomorrow," she declared.

Becoming a Public Figure

Benjamin's dedication and hard work first attracted national attention in 1995, when the *New York Times* published a long feature article about her. Her story was soon told in other national publications, and *Time* magazine named her one of "The Nation's 50 Leaders Age 40 and Under." Invitations to appear on "CBS This Morning" and "ABC World News Tonight" followed.

Benjamin's visibility within the medical profession also increased during this time. She had been a member of the American Medical Association (AMA), the country's leading professional organization for doctors, since her days in medical school. In 1986 she had even helped establish the AMA's Young Physician section to represent the concerns of doctors under the age of 40. But the publicity she garnered from newspaper and television coverage vaulted her to a leadership role in the organization. In 1995 she became the first African-American woman and the first physician under the age of 40 to become a member of the AMA's board of trustees. From her first day as a trustee, Benjamin used this position of influence to raise public awareness of the health needs of rural communities. "These people are being ignored, and I need to be their voice," she stated.

Benjamin gained an understanding of the importance of her appointment to the board in 1996, when she was attending her first AMA board meeting. As she strode through the hotel where the conference was taking place, an elderly, black hotel maintenance worker stopped to speak with her. "He said, 'I want you to know everybody in the hotel knows you're here, and we're very proud of you,'" recalled Benjamin. "That's when I realized the great responsibility of being in this position."

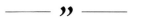

After Hurricane Georges destroyed her clinic, Benjamin confessed that "I just wanted to cry. A decade of work and all of our equipment, computers, records, everything down to the thermometers was destroyed."

Fellow board members say that Benjamin played a vital role in the board's work. "She gave us a perspective in her role as a young, solo, rural practitioner dedicated to educating her patients," stated Timothy Flaherty, the board's vice chairman. "Regina has unique skills, and she made the board more aware of and sensitive to minority issues. She was listened to very carefully."

Benjamin's influence continued to grow in the late 1990s. In 1997 she was inducted into the Institute of Medicine (IOM), an elite organization that advises the federal government on policy issues involving medicine and health care. She also served as president of the AMA's Education and Research Foundation from 1997 to 1998. Finally, Benjamin was the recipient of the 1997 Nelson Mandela Award for Health and Human Rights, a prize given by the Kaiser Family Foundation in honor of Nelson Mandela, former president of South Africa and winner of the Nobel Peace Prize.

Rebuilding After Disaster Strikes

In the fall of 1998 Benjamin watched helplessly as her beloved clinic was destroyed by Hurricane Georges. "I just wanted to cry," she recalled. "A

When Hurricane Georges destroyed her clinic, Benjamin used her pickup truck to make house calls to her many patients.

decade of work and all of our equipment, computers, records, everything down to the thermometers was destroyed. Mildew covered everything, and the stench was sickening. . . . Luckily, nobody died. In the end we were grateful for that."

Benjamin's insurance covered only the cost of replacing damaged medical records. Everything else would have to be replaced out of her own pocketbook. But Benjamin stepped up to the daunting task with her usual optimism. She secured a loan from the Small Business Administration and started rebuilding her clinic in a different location. She also dried her patients' files in the sun for months to save them. And even as she set about rebuilding her clinic, she continued to meet the medical needs of the surrounding community. She turned her 1988 Ford pickup into a mobile medical treatment unit, treating patients in this way for two years until she could reopen the clinic. "You can't just quit taking care of people who need you," Benjamin explained. "There was no one else to see them."

Benjamin's dedication to serving her patients never wavered, despite the long hours she spent behind the wheel of her truck. "I hope I make a difference one person at a time," she stated. "By making a patient feel better, by being able to tell a mother that her baby is going to be okay. Whether her baby is four or 44 the look on the mother's face is the same. I also hope that I am making a difference in my community by providing a clinic where patients can come and receive health care with dignity."

Trying to Make a Difference

Today, Benjamin is routinely consulted by state and national medical associations who are interested in setting up clinics like hers in other parts of the country. A severe need exists for such facilities. Although nearly a quarter of the American population lives in rural areas, fewer than one out of 10 medical school graduates set up their practices in rural areas. Benjamin is also one of 85 small town Alabama doctors who annually host medical students from the University of Alabama Medical School in an effort to get them interested in rural health care.

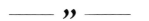

"I hope I make a difference one person at a time. By making a patient feel better, by being able to tell a mother that her baby is going to be okay. Whether her baby is four or 44 the look on the mother's face is the same."

Since her work in Bayou LaBatre began attracting notice, Benjamin has received a number of high-paying job offers from hospitals and medical practices in urban areas. But she has steadfastly refused to leave her clinic. As the community's only physician, she knows that people in and around Bayou LaBatre depend on her. "I practice here mainly because I like the people and feel I am needed," she declared. "I did not enter medicine for its financial rewards, so money has never been an important consideration in how or where I practice."

In recent years, Benjamin's efforts to improve the health of the people of Bayou LaBatre have led her to establish a variety of community education programs and initiatives. For example, she has persuaded many fishermen in the region to stop polluting the waters of the bayous with their used motor oil. She has also convinced local factory owners to provide their workers with safer and healthier workplace conditions. Benjamin even established an adult literacy program in the town. The program was badly needed, since 30 percent of the residents belong to families that emigrated from Vietnam, Laos, and Cambodia. "She helps a hell of a lot of people

Benjamin hugs a relative of one of her many patients during a house call.

down here," said one wheelchair-bound citizen. "She's as good a person as she is a doctor."

In 2002 Benjamin helped found the Southern Center for Health Care Access, a group of "safety net" hospitals that are willing to treat patients who have no insurance and cannot afford medical care. That same year, she became the first African-American president of the Medical Association of the State of Alabama. Louis W. Sullivan, who served as U.S. Secretary of Health and Human Services from 1989 to 1993, praised the choice. "Regina not only provides health care in an underserved area, but she's a role model and a community leader," he said.

In addition to her many clinic responsibilities, Benjamin is an associate dean for rural health at the University of South Alabama College of Medicine in Mobile. "That income and a lot of credit card debt keep me and the clinic going," she said. But despite the tight financial situation, she is optimistic about expanding the clinic's hours and services. In fact, she has plans to hire a second doctor for the clinic. According to Benjamin, the help-wanted advertisement will declare: "Long hours, low pay, great job satisfaction, and all the shrimp and oysters you can eat."

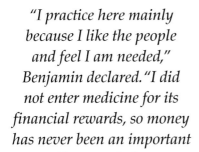

> *"I practice here mainly because I like the people and feel I am needed,"* Benjamin declared. *"I did not enter medicine for its financial rewards, so money has never been an important consideration in how or where I practice."*

HOME AND FAMILY

Benjamin lives in a ranch home in Spanish Fort, which is near Bayou LaBatre. "This area feels like home to me," she said. "There's no better place than home. And there's such a need here. I feel appreciated and needed." She is single, although her patients are doing their best to put an end to that. "They're always matchmaking," she admitted with a smile. "But it never works out."

HOBBIES AND OTHER INTERESTS

When Benjamin is not working at the clinic, she enjoys shooting pool and skydiving. She also has done missionary work in Honduras, and is very interested in adventure travel.

HONORS AND AWARDS

Woman of the Year ("CBS This Morning"): 1996
Nelson Mandela Award for Health and Human Rights (Kaiser Family Foundation): 1997
Morehouse School of Medicine Award for Excellence in Primary Care: 2002

FURTHER READING

Books

Contemporary Black Biography, Vol. 20, 1998

Periodicals

Ebony, Mar. 1997, p.86
Good Housekeeping, Sep. 2003, p.117
Modern Healthcare, May 22, 2000, p.34
New York Times, Apr. 3, 1995, p.A12
People Weekly, May 13, 2002, p.219
Reader's Digest, Jan. 2003, p.15

Redbook, Oct. 2001, p.86
Southern Living, June 1999, p.130

Online Articles

http://www.nlm.nih.gov/changingthefaceofmedicine/physicians/
    biography_31.html
    (*National Library of Medicine,* "Regina Benjamin," undated)

ADDRESS

Dr. Regina Benjamin
Bayou LaBatre Rural Health Clinic
13833 Tapia Lane
Bayou LaBatre, AL 36509

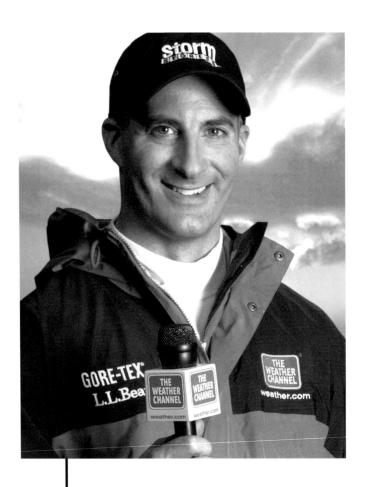

Jim Cantore 1964-

American Meteorologist
Host of "Storm Stories" and Other Programming on
the Weather Channel

BIRTH

James Donald Cantore (pronounced Can-TOR-ee) III was
born February 16, 1964, in Waterbury, Connecticut. His father,
James, worked for the U.S. Postal Service. His mother, Betty,
was a homemaker. He is the oldest of four adopted children.
Cantore has one younger brother, Vincent, and two younger
sisters, Paula and Carol.

YOUTH

Cantore spent his earliest years in Beacon Falls, Connecticut, but his family moved to White River Junction, Vermont, when he was still a youngster. Cantore's Vermont childhood gave him ample opportunity to sample the full range of weather extremes, from sweltering summer days to bone-chilling winter storms. The weather soon became a source of fascination to him, especially when storm systems swept over the horizon. In fact, one of Cantore's most vivid childhood memories involves a vacation trip to Virginia in which he witnessed towering thunderstorms rolling over Chesapeake Bay.

——— **"** ———

As Cantore grew older, he spent a lot of his free time studying the weather. He was encouraged by his father, who was proud of his oldest son's curiosity. "Dad didn't get too mad when he found me on the porch in my shorts at 2 a.m. shoveling the new-fallen snow, or when 10 friends would call in the morning to ask me if we would have school that day," he remarked.

——— **"** ———

As Cantore grew older, he spent a lot of his free time studying the weather. He was encouraged by his father, who was proud of his oldest son's curiosity. "Dad didn't get too mad when he found me on the porch in my shorts at 2 a.m. shoveling the new-fallen snow, or when 10 friends would call in the morning to ask me if we would have school that day," he remarked. Even in those early days of his youth, Cantore became known as the community's self-taught weatherman.

Cantore even came to view mid-February snowstorms as a sort of birthday treat especially for him. "It was like a present to me," he recalled. Cantore's favorite birthday storm came on his 14th birthday. That year, a tremendous blizzard roared across New England, creating massive 25-foot snowdrifts in some parts of Vermont. Cantore's school promptly called a snow day, enabling him to spend the entire day frolicking in the drifts.

EDUCATION

Cantore posted good grades at Hartford High School. He particularly enjoyed science and math courses, including biology, physics, and calculus. After graduating from high school in 1982, Cantore enrolled at Lyndon

Cantore has spent his entire career as a meteorologist on The Weather Channel.

State College in Lyndonville, Vermont, where he focused on science and communications courses.

A pivotal event in Cantore's schooling came in 1985, during his junior year at Lyndon. He enrolled in a speech class titled "Oral Interpretation," in which students were encouraged to act out scenes from movies, stories from books, or other works that lent themselves to public speaking. When Cantore's turn arrived, he delivered a detailed weather forecast for his classmates. As the semester progressed, he delivered a series of forecasts. By the end of the semester, he had even incorporated weather maps into his presentations to simulate the experience of being a television weatherman. Cantore enjoyed the exercise so much that he became convinced that he should pursue a career in meteorology. To this day he credits Terry Portner, the instructor of the class, for her support. "She let me focus on what I loved," Cantore declared.

Seizing on the opportunity to perform weather forecasts in front of a real camera, Cantore also became a regular presence on a small television station owned and operated by Lyndon State. After his junior year, Cantore also took a summer internship with the weather department of a major television station in Boston. He did not make any on-camera appearances during this time, but he did gain valuable experience in weather tracking and in operating the graphics machines used by television forecasters.

Cantore graduated with a bachelor of science degree from Lyndon State College in 1986.

CAREER HIGHLIGHTS

Upon graduating from college, Cantore was confident that he would be able to find a job as a television meteorologist. After all, Lyndon State's communications department had an excellent reputation, and he knew that agents and recruiters often contacted the school looking for potential on-air personalities. Cantore's confidence proved well-founded. He fielded job offers from television stations across the country, including stations located in cities like Yakima, Washington, and Twin Falls, Idaho.

But before he had the chance to consider any of these positions, Cantore received an intriguing job offer from a new national cable television station called the Weather Channel (TWC). This station, which featured weather forecasts around the clock, wanted him to be one of their primary on-air personalities. Cantore jumped at the offer, which seemed like a dream come true for any meteorologist. "I am proud to say the Weather Channel was my first job out of college," he later declared.

"I never consider a day at work a day at work," said Cantore. "I love what I do. When you're thinking about starting a career, make sure it's doing something you love."

A Familiar Face

Cantore made his first appearance on the Weather Channel in July 1986. He quickly became one of the most recognizable faces on the station. It seemed like viewers could tune in at any time—morning, night, weekends—and see Cantore standing in front of a map, giving forecasts and explaining weather phenomena for regions all across the United States. "The schedule was brutal, but valuable," he recalled. "I got a chance to hone my skills and get good in a hurry." The rigorous demands of his schedule never caused him to doubt his chosen career path, either. "I never consider a day at work a day at work," he said. "I love what I do. When you're thinking about starting a career, make sure it's doing something you love."

In the late 1980s, the Weather Channel chose Cantore to host a variety of programs designed to entertain as well as educate viewers about the weather. Notable specials of this type included "Wildfire," which focused on the fires that scorched Yellowstone National Park in 1987. He also hosted the "Fall Foliage Report," a program that was broadcast every autumn in the late 1980s and 1990s. But Cantore did not really attract the attention of the American public until he emerged as the Weather Channel's leading "reporter on the scene" during severe weather events.

Beginning in the early 1990s, Cantore reported live from virtually every major weather event that rocked the United States, including hurricanes Andrew, Fran, Georges, Floyd, Mitch, and Bonnie. He also covered the incredible ice storm that battered New England in 1998, as well as the 1999 Chicago blizzard, which registered the second heaviest snowfall in the city's history. With each passing year, growing numbers of viewers turned to the Weather Channel as their primary source of information on major storms. "Viewers have told us, 'You can show us 100 maps, but we want to see what the weather is like,'" explained Cantore. This heightened exposure gradually transformed Cantore into one of the country's best-known meteorologists.

"We want to go out where the story is," stated Cantore. "I would rather cover a hurricane than anything else. I'd like to see a Category 5 storm someday. I want to see just how powerful it is."

Cantore enjoyed each and every one of these assignments, despite the danger involved. "I'm begging for that stuff," he said. "We want to go out where the story is. . . . I would rather cover a hurricane than anything else. I'd like to see a Category 5 storm [the most powerful class of hurricane] someday. I want to see just how powerful it is. I've seen pictures of a hot dog that went through a door. Seriously. I'm not kidding." But while Cantore acknowledged that he feels a definite "adrenaline rush" when he is the middle of a hurricane or blizzard, he never loses sight of the fact that a storm event is a serious issue for those who are caught in its path. "I always remember the people, their homes, and how much is at stake," he said.

In the Eye of the Storm

The first major storm that Cantore covered on-location was Hurricane Andrew in 1992. The experience proved to be a harsh introduction to the world of extreme weather. Cantore and a crew were dispatched to Baton Rouge, Louisiana, for the second landfall of Andrew, which had already

Cantore's job takes him to storm sites all across the country.

devastated Homestead, Florida. They arrived in advance of the hurricane and settled into their hotel rooms for the night. Cantore and his crew were sound asleep when fierce winds hit the area. The blasts were so strong that the air conditioning unit in Cantore's room blew in right through the window. Cantore quickly joined his colleagues, all of whom had been awakened by the roaring storm. By 4:00 in the morning Cantore and the rest of the crew were providing live coverage of the devastating hurricane.

Cantore's most dangerous storm experience, however, came during Hurricane Fran, which rocked the Atlantic seaboard in September 1996. "I was positioned on the land side of the causeway one mile inland at Wrightsville Beach in North Carolina and the storm was amazingly strong and we were being pelted by stones and hard rain," he recalled. "That was pretty intense."

Cantore never failed to be impressed by the fury of these major storm events. On a couple of occasions, however, Cantore has felt more endangered from emotional storm victims than from the weather itself. "I was once in Linden, Kansas, running after a tornado," he recalled. "Two women came up, each holding a shotgun. They weren't the least bit happy to see our crew. They wanted to make sure that we didn't give their address on TV. Their home had been destroyed and they were afraid of looters. I gulped, then told them, 'Yup, fine. You've got it.' And then we packed

Cantore loves reporting on the weather, but his coverage reflects an understanding of the severe toll that storms can take on people's lives.

up and headed out." During another assignment, Cantore stated that he "was tracking a storm in Tampa when a man came out of his house, started pounding me in the chest, then turned around and left. I know that weather people are blamed for the weather, but I still can't figure that one out."

Challenges of Storm Coverage

As they track each severe storm event, Cantore and his colleagues seek to strike an appropriate balance in their coverage. "We want to inform our viewers about the potential impact of the weather events so they can protect their property and most importantly, their lives, but we don't want to be part of the news story," Cantore stated. "We locate ourselves close enough to the action to help viewers understand the severity of the weather, but stay out of harm's way." In fact, while covering Hurricane Isabel in September 2003, he issued an apology to viewers for straying too close to a set of waves pounding the shoreline while taping a segment to air on TWC later that day.

In recent years, Cantore has also had to deal with a growing field of competitors. When he and other Weather Channel meteorologists first started providing live coverage of major weather events, they were usually the first—and often the only—media outlet to provide "on the scene" coverage. But as media interest in these events has grown, Cantore and his crew now find that they have to fight other broadcast competitors for satellite truck space and dramatic video footage. Weather Channel personnel covering storms also have to plan carefully to ensure that their reports reach their intended audience. "You can't just stand out in front of these things and try to broadcast," Cantore explained. "If the winds are too strong, you start shaking the satellite dish around, forget it. Nobody's going to get a signal."

There have also been a few occasions when Cantore has rushed to a potential storm site, only to find that the weather system he was anticipating had changed course or failed to develop. "It's not uncommon for a fast-developing storm to dissipate quickly," he explained. For example, in early 2001 a blizzard narrowly missed the New York metropolitan area. "I'm kind of discouraged the storm didn't pan out the way we thought it would," Cantore admitted. "There might be as many as 8 inches of snow on the ground in the New York area, but that's not nearly as bad as we thought. We were expecting 28 inches."

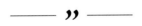

"You can't just stand out in front of these [storms] and try to broadcast," Cantore explained. "If the winds are too strong, you start shaking the satellite dish around, forget it. Nobody's going to get a signal."

Beyond the Weather

In 1999 Cantore was selected by the FOX television network to join its popular NFL pregame show. Each Sunday, Cantore provided weather forecasts for football games that would be played in outdoor stadiums later in the day. Cantore still has fond memories of his season on the show. "That was the best gig in television. That was so much fun," he said. Cantore's experience on the FOX pregame show also paved the way for him to showcase his talents on a range of other programs. Over the last several years he has reported on a variety of high-profile events, from the Space Shuttle Discovery launch to the Winter X Games.

But despite his professional success in other areas of television, Cantore still devotes most of his time to weather-related programming. In 2002 he was named host of "Atmospheres," an educational news magazine that took him all around the world to report on brave men and women whose

In addition to his reporting responsibilities, Cantore serves as host of the TWC programs "Atmospheres" and "Storm Stories."

careers expose them to the forces of nature. The program also educated viewers about communities where livelihoods depend on regional weather systems.

Since January 2003 Cantore has also appeared as host of "Storm Stories," a new Weather Channel program that highlights the real-life experiences of people trapped in dangerous storm events. "This show is for anybody who's just in awe of the weather," Cantore said. "It takes a look at the human element in any dramatic event like hurricanes, tornadoes, and floods." Many of the shows feature actual video footage from the events chronicled, while others re-create events using actors. Cantore is proud of the show, which is one of the Weather Channel's most popular programs. "The way I look at it is it's probably the most real reality TV you could get," he said. "It's a once in a lifetime experience for so many people, and a life-changing experience. As long as you and I are on this Earth, we will never be able to tell all the stories. Everyone's got a storm story or two or three."

Cantore is also a frequent guest meteorologist on network news programs, including MSNBC's "The News with Brian Williams." Unless he is on assignment to cover a storm on-location, Cantore reports nightly from the Atlanta studios on the Weather Channel's "Evening Edition" program. During these telecasts he and his fellow on-air meteorologists play the role of "StormTracker," tracing and explaining new weather developments around the country.

An Electrifying Personality

Cantore's hard work and dedication have put him at the forefront of today's weather reporters. In fact, his energetic, authoritative on-air personality has garnered him admirers from all walks of life. For example, NASCAR driver Bobby Labonte has admitted to being hooked on the Weather Channel—and on Cantore's reports in particular. The two have since formed a friendship. "Jim has asked me to come out to Oklahoma to chase tornadoes with him," Labonte once remarked.

Tucker Barnes, the founder of a popular severe weather Internet site called www.wildweather.com, also testifies to Cantore's popularity with viewers. "I'm not sure if there's an official fan club," said Barnes, "but we get several hundred pieces of mail a week, asking us to profile this meteorologist or that meteorologist—and our number one request is Jim Cantore. A lot of females find him very attractive and sort of manly—a Harrison Ford-type swashbuckler, taking on nature." For his part, Cantore admits that the attention he receives is flattering, but he claims that "the people that like to hang out with me are the people that love the weather and kind of feed off my passion for the weather."

> *"The people that like to hang out with me are the people that love the weather and kind of feed off my passion for the weather."*

Finally, Cantore enjoys the respect of his colleagues at the network and in the meteorological community. "We say it all the time behind his back. When Cantore is on, whether from a weather event or in the studio, his passion just raises the energy level of everybody near him," declared one Weather Channel executive. "Jim would go out on all the weather events if we let him." Barnes, meanwhile, described him as a forecaster who is "both affable and extremely weather savvy. The man has been blessed with the ability to at once inform, educate, and entertain his viewers in a three-minute segment."

MARRIAGE AND FAMILY

Cantore met his wife Tamra in 1987, a year after joining the Weather Channel. They wed in 1990. They have a home near Atlanta, Georgia, where they live with their two children, Christina and Benjamin. "They love to see me on television," Cantore said, "and I think it's great that they can. Especially when I'm on the road for days at a time."

HOBBIES AND OTHER INTERESTS

Cantore enjoys a wide range of outdoor pursuits, including golf, softball, skiing, and running, all of which help him when he's out on assignment covering a severe weather situation. "You have to stay in shape for this job," he said. "It's like my little marathon. I like to see how long I can stay up and give a quality broadcast. It gets exhausting, just being out there getting beaten. One time I forgot where I was. It's a humbling experience." He is also a big NASCAR racing fan.

Cantore is an avid supporter of several major charities. He has contributed time and energy to organizations such as the Juvenile Diabetes Walk for the Cure, the Dana Farber Cancer Institute, and the Girls and Boys Club. One particular charity that is very dear to Cantore's heart is the Michael J. Fox Foundation. This organization works to find treatments for Parkinson's disease, which Tamra Cantore has been diagnosed with. She has raised more than $75,000 for the Foundation, a sum which the meteorologist referred to as "a testament to my better half." Cantore also has taken steps to nurture aspiring meteorologists. He has announced plans to start an annual weekend weather workshop for students at Lyndon State College in the fall of 2004.

HONORS AND AWARDS

David S. Johnson Award (National Oceanic and Atmospheric
    Administration): 2003

FURTHER READING

Periodicals

Atlanta Journal-Constitution, Oct. 4, 2002, p.A1
Broadcasting and Cable, Sep. 29, 2003, p.36
Denver Rocky Mountain News, Dec. 9, 1999, p.A44
Green Bay (WI) Press-Gazette, May 2, 2002, p. B1
New York Post, June 1, 2003, p.8

New York Times, Aug. 28, 1998, p.A20; Apr. 28, 2002, p.8
Newark (NJ) Star-Ledger, Mar. 6, 2001, p.11
Orlando Sentinel, Sep. 23, 1999, p.E1
St. Petersburg Times, Sep. 10, 2003, Section 2, p.10
Washington Post, Sep. 29, 2003, p.D4
Wilmington (NC) Morning Star, Aug. 28, 1999, p.B1
USA Today, Mar. 7, 2001, p.A4; July 16, 2003, p.A3

Online Articles

http://www.cbs.com/
  (*CBS.com*, "Look Out Survivor!" Jan. 3, 2003)
http://www.charleston.net/
  (*Charleston Post and Courier Online*, "Weather Channel Revisits Hugo on
  'Storm Stories,'" Sep. 14, 2003)
http://www.charlotte.com/
  (*Charlotte Observer Online*, "If Storm Reporter Goes, They Follow,"
  Sep. 18, 2003)
http://www.publicaffairs.noaa.gov/
  (*NOAA Office of Public and Constituent and Intergovernmental Affairs*,
  "Weather Channel Meteorologist Receives NOAA-David Johnson
  Award," Apr. 9, 2003)
http://www.skinorthcarolina.com
  (*SkiNorthCarolina.com*, "Weather Is in His Blood . . . Jim Cantore of the
  Weather Channel," Mar. 14, 2003)
http://www.wildweather.com
  (*WildWeather.com*, "Jim Cantore: Meteorologist of the Month," Aug.
  2000)

ADDRESS

Jim Cantore
The Weather Channel
300 Interstate North Parkway
Atlanta, GA 30339

WORLD WIDE WEB SITE

http://www.weather.com/

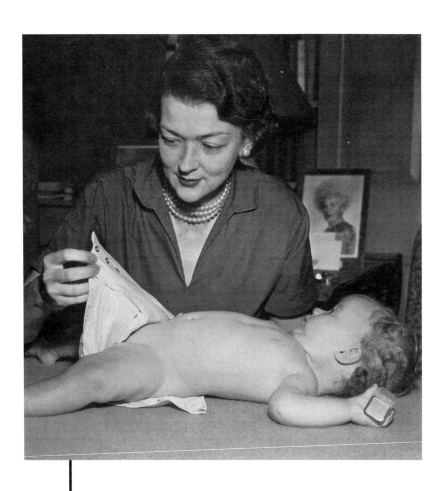

RETROSPECTIVE

Marion Donovan 1917-1998

American Inventor
Businesswoman Who Revolutionized Diaper Design

BIRTH

Marion Donovan was born Marion O'Brien on October 15, 1917, in South Bend, Indiana. Her father, Miles O'Brien, was an Irish immigrant who started a machine shop called South Bend Lathe Works with his twin brother John in 1906. Little is known about her mother, who died when Marion was seven years old. Marion was an only child.

YOUTH

After her mother's death, Marion maintained a very close relationship with her father. She spent countless hours hanging around both him and her uncle John as they managed the South Bend Lathe Works. Miles and John O'Brien had emigrated to the United States from Ireland in the 1870s. Encouraged by famed inventor Thomas Edison to pursue engineering careers, the twins attended Purdue University in West Lafayette, Indiana. They then used their college education and practical experience to design an improved lathe, one of the most essential tools of any machine shop. A lathe rotates a piece of material, such as wood or metal, around a horizontal axis and shapes it with fixed cutting tools.

The twins started their own lathe manufacturing company in 1906. They marketed their lathes across the country and even wrote an enormously popular guidebook about lathe usage. By 1930, when Marion Donovan was 13 years old, South Bend Lathe Works manufactured nearly half of the industrial lathes in the United States.

Marion admired her father's inventiveness and smart business sense. Inspired by his example, she spent many hours of her childhood tinkering with the tools available in the machine shop. Indeed, Marion applied her creative skills at a very young age, creating a "tooth powder" for cleaning teeth while in elementary school. Her father died in 1936, but her uncle lived for another 10 years. The company they founded together remains in operation to this day.

EDUCATION

A bright, curious student, Donovan completed high school in Indiana. She then moved east to attend Rosemont College, a Catholic women's college located in the suburbs of Philadelphia, Pennsylvania. She graduated with a bachelor of arts degree in English literature in 1939. Years later, after embarking on a successful business career, she returned to school. She graduated in 1958 from Yale University in New Haven, Connecticut, with a master's degree in architecture.

FIRST JOBS

After earning her bachelor's degree in 1939, Donovan accepted a job as an assistant editor at *Vogue* magazine in New York City. She also worked briefly in the editorial department at *Harper's Bazaar,* another national fashion magazine based in New York. In 1942 she married a leather importer named James Donovan. Like many other young married women of the era, Donovan decided to leave her job and focus on raising a family. The young couple moved to Westport, Connecticut, where they eventually had three children. As it turned out, however, motherhood rekindled Donovan's childhood enthusiasm for creative inventions.

CAREER HIGHLIGHTS

Like other young American mothers, Donovan came to regard many of her everyday chores as tiresome and exasperating. She became particularly frustrated by her diaper-changing responsibilities. Back in the early 1940s, when Donovan was raising her oldest children, mothers had no other option but to use cloth diapers and rubber diaper covers. But these materials were not convenient or easy to use. Donovan, for example, came to feel that whenever she laid her infant daughter down for a nap, she would immediately wet through her diaper and onto the crib sheets. The baby would then awaken, forcing Donovan to change and wash the sheets and hunt down a new diaper. In addition, the rubber diaper covers that were commonly used during this period functioned very poorly. They often leaked and trapped moisture on her baby's tender bottom, causing diaper rash. By the end of each day, Donovan

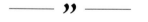

> *At the end of every day, Donovan's baby left her with a pile of wet laundry and smelly diapers. "I knew what everyone meant about the frustration with wet clothing," said Donovan. "It was a horrible, arduous job to deal with."*

found herself with a damp pile of laundry and smelly diapers to clean. "I knew what everyone meant about the frustration with wet clothing. It was a horrible, arduous job to deal with," Donovan stated. "I just wanted to contain the wet from going everywhere."

One day, Donovan eyed her lightweight and waterproof shower curtain in a new light. Reasoning that this material might be ideal for trapping moisture, she cut and sewed it into a diaper cover. She then cut her way through a series of shower curtains, trying various patterns. After experimenting for nearly three years, she created a leak-proof diaper cover out of nylon parachute material. Not only did the diaper cover reduce her laundry chores, it also eliminated the danger of accidentally jabbing her babies with the safety pins that held cloth diapers in place. Jabbing long safety pins through thick folds of diapers was no easy task. The pins had

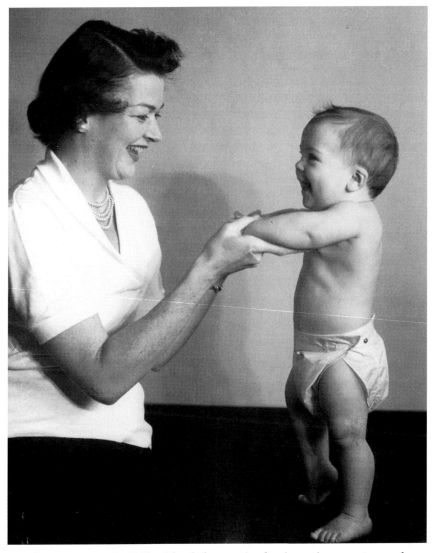

Donovan poses in 1949 with a baby wearing her invention, a waterproof outer cover for diapers called the "Boater."

to be pushed with real force and would sometimes slip through suddenly, poking the baby's tender skin. The snaps on Donovan's diaper cover eliminated the need for safety pins altogether. She dubbed her diaper cover "the Boater" because she said it kept the baby "afloat."

Donovan knew that other mothers could benefit from her design. Yet when she approached manufacturers with her idea, no one was interested. Unde-

45

terred, Donovan decided to finance her efforts herself. She formed a company called Donovan Enterprises to market her invention. In 1949 her diaper cover debuted on the shelves of the Saks Fifth Avenue department store in New York City. Selling for $1.95, the Boater became an instant success. Donovan's daughter, Christine, noted that within weeks of the Boater's appearance on store shelves, "orders poured in from department stores across the country as word spread that the invention 'revolutionized' parents' problems with their babies' soggy diapers."

Pursuing Other Inventions

In 1951 Donovan secured four patents for her ingenious invention. A short time later, she sold Donovan Enterprises and her diaper cover patents to another company for $1 million. But the sale of Donovan's business did not mean the end of her inventing days. In fact, the Boater was just the first of many new product ideas Donovan developed over the years. After selling her diaper cover business, for example, she immediately turned her energies to the development of a disposable paper diaper.

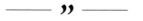

> *Donovan finally settled on a type of paper that was strong enough to handle hours of toddler activities, yet absorbent enough to carry moisture away.*

Donovan wanted to get rid of the mountains of soggy diapers women washed each day or bundled for a diaper service to clean. But she also knew that mothers would never accept a product that would make babies prone to diaper rash. Donovan thus experimented with a range of absorbent papers that wicked moisture away from the baby's bottom. She eventually settled upon a type of paper that was strong enough to handle hours of toddler activities, yet absorbent enough to carry moisture away from a baby's skin.

Donovan then approached several paper manufacturers with her idea. She was dismayed to find that all of the industry executives—primarily men who had little experience changing diapers—believed that her product would not be particularly popular with young mothers. They claimed that without heavy consumer demand, producing Donovan's disposable diapers would be too expensive. This viewpoint seems silly today, since disposable diapers are regularly used by virtually all American mothers. But industry resistance to disposable diapers remained strong for another decade. In 1961 Proctor & Gamble began mass-marketing Pampers dispos-

In 1951 Donovan sold her diaper cover patents to another company in exchange for $1 million.

able diapers, opening a market that eventually turned disposable diapers into a multi-billion dollar business.

Feeding Her Curiosity

According to all who knew her, Donovan's head buzzed with ideas for improving the tasks of daily life. Her daughter Christine claimed that her mother possessed an "insatiable curiosity," and said that she was "always vigilant in addressing a problem that only she thought was a problem." Sometimes, however, Donovan recognized that pursuing her invention ideas required more technical knowledge than she possessed. With this in mind, she returned to college, earning a master's degree in architecture from Yale University at the age of 41. She was one of three women in her graduating class. Her studies gave her engineering skills that proved valuable in her career as an inventor. In addition, her years at Yale gave her the expertise to design and build her dream home in Greenwich, Connecticut. She settled there with her second husband, John Butler.

Donovan spent the rest of her life working to find convenient solutions for everyday problems. She eventually obtained patents for more than a dozen inventions, including a space-saving hanger called "The Big Hang-Up" that was capable of holding up to 30 items. Another Donovan device was the "Zippity-Do," an elastic cord that enabled women to pull up zippers along the back of their dresses. Other inventions included a combined check book and ledger called the "Ledger Check," a soap dish that drained into household sinks, and a handy loop of dental floss called the "DentaLoop."

Throughout her long career, Donovan involved herself in every aspect of the invention process, including product development, machinery design, and marketing. She traveled to various factories in the United States and around the world to get machinery design ideas. She refined her ideas by corresponding with companies that specialized in areas her products would benefit, and she tirelessly promoted her inventions. She also worked as a product development consultant for other companies for many years. Donovan worked in all these capacities until her second husband suffered a stroke. She stopped working to care for him until his death in July 1998. She died four months later on November 4, 1998.

> ——— " ———
>
> *Throughout her long career, Donovan involved herself in every aspect of invention, including product development, machinery design, and marketing. She traveled around the world to get machinery design ideas, and she tirelessly promoted her inventions.*
>
> ——— " ———

An energetic and creative woman, Marion Donovan left a legacy for which all parents should be grateful. A record of her accomplishments can be found in the Archives Center of the Smithsonian Institution's National Museum of American History in Washington, D.C. The archives include design ideas, letters, patents, photos, and other materials that trace the many innovations Donovan pursued over the years. The Smithsonian Institution also displays her Boater diaper cover and several other Donovan inventions at its national museum in Washington, D.C.

MARRIAGE AND FAMILY

Donovan married James Donovan, a leather importer, in 1942. They eventually had three children—daughters Christine and Sharon and son James, Jr. She was later married to John Butler.

FURTHER READING

Books

Carey, Charles W., Jr. *American Biographies: American Inventors, Entrepreneurs, and Business Visionaries,* 2002

McClure, Judy. *Remarkable Women: Past and Present, Theoreticians and Builders: Mathematicians, Physical Scientists, Inventors,* 2000

Vare, Ethlie, and Greg Ptacek. *Mothers of Invention, From the Bra to the Bomb: Forgotten Women and Their Unforgettable Ideas,* 1987

Periodicals

Good Housekeeping, Sep. 1984, p.72

Milwaukee Journal Sentinel, Oct. 18, 1998, p.6

New York Times, Nov. 18, 1998, p.B15

South Bend Tribune, Nov. 22, 1998, p.B1

Online Articles

http://americanhistory.si.edu/archives/d8721.htm
(*The Archives Center,* "Marion O'Brien Donovan Papers, 1949-1996," 2000)

http://www.ideafinder.com/history/inventors/donovan.htm
(*The Great Idea Finder,* "Marion Donovan: Fascinating Facts about Marion Donovan Inventor of Disposable Diapers in 1946," undated)

http://inventors.about.com/library/inventors/bldiaper.htm
(*About.com,* "Disposable Diapers—Marion Donovan," undated)

Michael Fay 1956-

American Conservation Biologist
Completed the Megatransect, a 15-Month, 2,000-Mile
Walk across Africa's Congo Basin
Inspired the Creation of 13 National Parks in Gabon

BIRTH

J. Michael Fay was born on September 19, 1956, in Plainfield,
New Jersey. He was the second of three sons born to James
Fay, who is a retired insurance agent, and his wife, who is a
homemaker.

YOUTH

The Fay family moved to Pasadena, California, when Michael was a baby. He loved nature and the outdoors from an early age. As a little boy, he would look out of his bedroom window and dream about exploring the San Gabriel Mountains he saw looming in the distance. By the time he was six years old, Fay was spending entire days wandering in the woods around his home. "I've always tried to go to the wildest places I can find," he explained. "I've always tried to be in nature."

Accompanied by his brothers or by neighborhood friends, Fay often watched animals, climbed rocks and trees, and poked around in old mine shafts from before dawn until after dark. "I just love exploring," he stated. "It's my greatest joy." On a few occasions Fay had to be rescued from high ledges or deep pits by emergency crews, but his zeal for adventure never dimmed. "I would be questioned by my parents," he recalled, "but since I always came home it was never an issue." Later in his childhood, Fay often climbed up in the foothills to an elevation of 7,000 feet in order to enjoy the clean air above the smog that enveloped Los Angeles.

"I just love exploring," said Fay. "I knew every nook and cranny of the woods from Summit [New Jersey] to the Pennsylvania border, and north to the Canadian border. . . . I must have been out [in the woods] 500 times and never saw anyone except the buddies I was with."

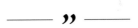

When Fay was 12 years old, his family moved back east to Summit, New Jersey. As before, Fay spent a great deal of time exploring his surroundings. "I knew every nook and cranny of the woods from Summit to the Pennsylvania border, and north to the Canadian border," he remembered. "I must have been out [in the woods] 500 times and never saw anyone except the buddies I was with." As a teenager, Fay spent two summers as a counselor at Camp Wanderlust in Maine, where he led groups of kids on wilderness fly-fishing and canoe trips. On many of these excursions, Fay's party would go several weeks without seeing other people.

EDUCATION

Fay attended Summit High School in New Jersey. He had trouble concentrating on subjects that did not interest him, so he only managed to earn average grades. During his senior year of high school, he took advantage of a program that allowed students to pursue a school-approved project rather than attend traditional classes. His project took him to Arizona, where he studied plant and animal life in the mountains for his final year of high school.

After graduating from Summit High in 1974, Fay returned to Arizona to attend college at the University of Arizona. He earned a bachelor of science degree in botany (the scientific study of plants) in 1978. During his undergraduate years, Fay spent two summers as a bird guide in Alaska. "I have always been a conservationist as far back as I can remember, and in college I fell in love with the big landscapes of Alaska," he recalled. "I thought I would end up there." But his life took a different turn later in 1978 when he joined the Peace Corps, a U.S. government program that sends American volunteers to developing countries to educate and assist local people.

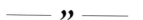

"I have always been a conservationist as far back as I can remember, and in college I fell in love with the big landscapes of Alaska," Fay recalled. "I thought I would end up there."

Fay spent the next six years working as a volunteer botanist on the savannas of Tunisia and the Central African Republic. The Peace Corps provided Fay with a small motorcycle that he used to explore roadless parts of the region. "I decided that the way to really see that place was to take long traverses from one road to another, sometimes 70 or 80 kilometers across the places where no one had been," he explained.

In 1984 Fay returned to the United States to continue his education at Washington University in St. Louis, Missouri. He also worked at the Missouri Botanical Garden during this time. In 1986 he earned his master's degree in anthropology, the scientific study of human origins and cultural development. Fay then returned to Africa to conduct field research for his doctoral degree. He spent the next two years studying western lowland gorillas in the tropical forests of the Central African Republic.

Fay returned to the United States in 1988 with the intention of completing his doctoral dissertation. But two months later he went back to Africa to conduct a field study of forest elephants in the Republic of Congo. As the research project progressed, Fay fell in love with the tropical forests of central Africa. In fact, he decided to dedicate his career to preserving them. His conservation efforts prevented him from completing his dissertation until 1997, when he finally earned his Ph.D. from Washington University.

CAREER HIGHLIGHTS

Changing Focus from Research to Conservation

Fay's love for Africa and its wildlife first developed during his years in the Peace Corps. But he found his true calling in the late 1980s, when he visited the tropical forests in the central part of the continent for the first time. As a doctoral candidate studying western lowland gorillas, Fay began exploring the forests of the Central African Republic on foot. He used a scientific research technique called a line transect survey—which involves moving through habitat in a straight line and collecting data along the way—to locate and count gorilla nests. He also followed groups of gorillas for days at a time in order to gather information about the food they ate and the territory they in-

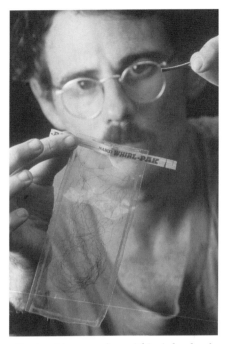

During his research on Africa's lowland gorillas, Fay used samples of hair at nesting sites to identify individual gorillas through their genetic "fingerprints."

habited. One of his most startling discoveries was that western lowland gorillas clap their hands as a means of communication.

As Fay studied the gorillas, he grew concerned about the future of their tropical forest habitat. "In the next ten years, most of the forest that gorillas live in will be opened up and exploited [for logging and farming]," he stated. "Gorillas will be nearly extinct in a decade if we don't do something to protect their habitat, and we literally know nothing about them."

Toward the end of 1988, Fay returned to Washington University with the intention of writing his doctoral dissertation on western lowland gorillas. But several weeks later, a respected elephant biologist named Richard Barnes asked him to go to the Republic of Congo in west-central Africa to conduct a survey of forest elephants. Forest elephants are a subspecies of the elephants found on the savannas of Africa. They are slightly smaller and have straighter tusks than their better-known relatives. Fay could not resist the opportunity to conduct further research in the forests of central Africa. He set aside his dissertation and traveled to the Congo in early 1989.

Fay did his elephant research project in a tract of uninhabited land in northern Congo. The Ndoki River ran along its western edge, hills bordered it to the north, and swamps protected it from the south and east. As a result of its inaccessibility, the area remained virtually untouched by humans. It was home to an abundance of wildlife that offered a goldmine of possibilities for scientific research, including 1,000 species of plants, 200 species of birds, and such endangered animals as forest elephants, lowland gorillas, chimpanzees, and leopards.

———— **"** ————

"We were doing studies on various species, and we saw a great need for conservation in the [African] forest," said Fay. "We saw abundant wildlife, amazing biological richness, and trees that were equivalent to any protected area in North America. . . . We thought it was crazy that there were no protected areas, and it prompted us to embark upon a mission."

———— **"** ————

As Fay explored the Ndoki region for his research project, he learned that it too was threatened by logging. Foreign-owned logging companies had already depleted surrounding areas of valuable timber, with disastrous effects on ecosystems and wildlife. Once the logging companies cut roads into previously inaccessible forest, poachers used the roads to kill wildlife to sell as bushmeat. As the wildlife disappeared, local people were forced to convert the forest into farmland to feed their families. The forest ecosystems were destroyed, but most of the financial benefits went to the international logging companies rather than to the local people. Fay was deeply distressed by this situation and grew determined to help protect the forests.

Establishing National Parks in the Congo Basin

Fay gradually changed the main focus of his career from science to conservation. He began working with other scientists, as well as such international organizations as the World Conservation Society (WCS) and the U.S. Agency for International Development (USAID), to protect areas of African forest by designating them as national parks. "We were doing studies on various species, and we saw a great need for conservation in the forest," he explained. "Traditionally, national parks were restricted to savanna environments in Africa — the big game parks. No one had thought about establishing parks in forest before. We saw abundant wildlife, amazing biological richness, and trees that were equivalent to any protected area in North America that's established because of the vegetation — like Sequoia

1 Akanda National Park

6 Monts De Cristal National Park

11 Minkébé National Park

G A B O N

Libreville

12 Mwagne National Park

2 Pongara National Park

8 Lopé National Park

10 Ivindo National Park

7 Waka National Park

9 Mont Birougou National Park

4 Moulakaba-Doudou National Park

3 Loango National Park

13 Plateaux Batéké National Park

5 Mayumba National Park

A F R I C A

GABON Congo Basin

This map of Gabon in Africa shows 13 national parks that Fay helped create.

National Park [in northern California]. We thought it was crazy that there were no protected areas, and it prompted us to embark upon a mission."

Fay's first conservation efforts were aimed at protecting the area where he completed his gorilla research project—the Dzanga-Sangha region of the southwestern Central African Republic. With the support of the WCS and other groups, he convinced leaders of the Central African Republic to set aside 1,700 square miles of tropical forest as Dzanga-Sangha National Park in 1990.

Fay agreed to serve as the acting director of Dzanga-Sangha until a permanent director could be found. In this position, he led efforts to protect the park's wildlife from poachers. Despite an international ban on ivory

Fay canoes down one of central Africa's many wild rivers.

trade that went into effect in 1989, large numbers of elephants were still being slaughtered for their tusks. Fay realized that local people were being paid to kill the park's elephants and supply their valuable ivory tusks to international dealers. His anti-poaching strategy involved paying local people to act as game wardens, so that they had incentive to protect the park's elephants rather than kill them. "We went into every village that was identified as a center of poaching. We said, 'Listen guys, there's a problem. There's lots of elephants being killed. We know you're killing them so let's try to solve this problem together,'" Fay remembered. "And that's exactly what we did. . . . We just went over to the shooters and said we think we can offer you more than you're getting now."

Also in 1990, Fay accepted a position as a field researcher for the Wildlife Conservation Society. Based at the Bronx Zoo in New York City, the WCS works to save wildlife and its habitat around the world and to promote sustainable interaction between humans and wildlife. After he completed his term as acting director of Dzanga-Sangha National Park in 1991, Fay was named director of a new conservation project that involved the WCS, other environmental groups, and the government of the Republic of Congo. The goal was to establish a wilderness reserve in the Ndoki region, where Fay had done his forest elephant research. This valuable tract of forest was located just across the Congolese border from Dzanga-Sangha National Park.

The main obstacle to creating a new national park in the Republic of Congo was the poverty and overpopulation affecting the country. Congolese leaders faced a great deal of pressure to exploit the country's natural resources in order to provide the people with a better standard of living. "The biggest problem is not the willingness of the people—from the lowliest Pygmy [an indigenous forest-dwelling people of central Africa] all the way up to the president—to create and endorse the parks," Fay noted. "That's the easy part. The problem is that the infrastructure in most of Africa is not maintained, not managed, because of a high rate of corruption and quickly growing human populations. Priorities are focused on immediate needs."

"What you see in these forests is something that you cannot see anywhere else on earth—nature without humans," said Fay. "People need to know that wild places are still out there. I want to know the forest, and the only way to do that is to walk it."

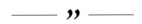

Fay surveyed the area of the proposed park himself, crossing its 70-mile expanse on foot multiple times. He also helped arrange funding from the WCS and other international sources. In late 1993 he finally succeeded in convincing the Congolese government to designate a one-million-acre area as Nouabalé-Ndoki National Park. Fay negotiated with the government, logging companies, and local people to create an innovative management plan for the new park. Under this plan, the central part of the park was set aside exclusively for scientific research and conservation-related activities. This central protected area was surrounded by a "buffer zone," in which environmentally friendly human uses—such as sustainable logging, subsistence hunting, and tourism—were allowed in order to provide revenue to local people.

Launching the Megatransect

Despite playing a pivotal role in the creation of two national parks, Fay still felt he should do more to protect Africa's tropical forests from destruction. He was particularly concerned about the Congo Basin rainforest, a 700,000-square-mile area (about seven times the size of California) that accounts for about one-fourth of the world's tropical forest area. In fact, the Congo Basin rainforest is the second-largest tropical forest in the world (after the Amazon of South America). It holds an amazing variety of plants and animals, including such endangered species as gorillas, forest elephants, chimpanzees, and leopards. Yet the Congo Basin rainforest faces significant threats from logging and other unsustainable land use practices. In fact, sections of forest twice the size of Rhode Island are destroyed each year.

————— " —————

"The objectives [of the Megatransact] are simple. I want to show the world that in Central Africa there remains a vast wilderness, sparsely populated, with the natural environment mainly intact, where biodiversity is overwhelming," stated Fay. "I want to help preserve as much of this magical world as possible."

————— " —————

In 1996 Fay flew a small plane over the Republic of Congo and Gabon in west-central Africa. From the air, he observed a large, intact swath of forest that stretched from the Oubangui River in northeastern Congo to the Atlantic Ocean on the west coast of Gabon. The following year he began planning an ambitious project to study this forest area and raise funds for its protection. Fay decided to walk the entire 1,200-mile length of the forest corridor. He planned to survey the trees, wildlife, and human impacts he saw along the way. "What you see in these forests is something that you cannot see anywhere else on earth—nature without humans," he explained. "People need to know that wild places are still out there. I want to know the forest, and the only way to do that is to walk it."

Fay spent the next two years planning for what he described as "the longest forest walk ever." He called his project the "Megatransect"—from the terms "mega," meaning big, and "transect," referring to the line transect method of scientific research. He designed a route that would pass through the deepest part of the forest, remaining as far as possible from human settlements. He also convinced the WCS and the National Geographic Society to provide funding for the project.

In outlining his goals for the Megatransect, Fay stated that: "The objectives are simple. I want to show the world that in Central Africa there remains a vast wilderness, sparsely populated, with the natural environment mainly intact, where biodiversity is overwhelming. I want to document what this

During Fay's Megatransact, he used a video camera to document the presence of a wide assortment of wildlife.

forest contains: how many elephants and gorillas it shelters; the species and sizes of trees that grow there; the places where humans are found and where they are not. My goal: to understand the intricate web we call an ecosystem, to make sense of nature's incredibly complex jigsaw puzzle. Most of all, I want to help preserve as much of this magical world as possible. I hope the knowledge gained from my experience will be used to muster the money it will take to save a few more million of these precious acres. This is my dream."

Walking through the Jungles of Africa

Fay officially launched the Megatransect on September 20, 1999, the day after his 43rd birthday. Over the course of the next 15 months, he ended up walking nearly 2,000 miles—the equivalent of traveling across the United States from Boston, Massachusetts, to Denver, Colorado. But the only roads he had to follow were elephant trails through the jungle. In fact, his course took him through areas so remote that the wildlife had apparently never encountered humans before. This "naive" wildlife reacted to Fay with curiosity rather than fear.

Fay hired two different teams of 10 to 12 Ba'Aka and Bambendjelle Pygmies to help clear a path, carry equipment, set up campsites, and prepare meals during the Megatransect. One group assisted him on the Congo portion of the trip, and the other group on the Gabon portion of the journey. As a result, Fay was the only person to complete the entire walk. His attire for the journey was a pair of quick-drying river shorts and Teva sport sandals. His equipment included a digital video camera, an audio recorder, a still camera, a hand-held computer, and a global positioning system (GPS) that took a reading on his exact position every 20 seconds. Fay and his team also carried a satellite telephone, which enabled them to call and report their position so that they could receive food and other supplies by airdrop. They refrained from hunting during the Megatransect because they did not want to disrupt the behavior patterns of the naive wildlife.

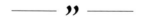

"We're having a great time," Fay wrote. "Been out on the trail for eight weeks now, walking through the mud, chopping our way through the rough patches. The forest is keeping us busy with elephants, chimpanzees, monkeys, monitor lizards, aardvarks, hinge tortoises, and tons of other wildlife. We're arrived in a place called Goualougo. . . . We've dubbed it the Last Place on Earth because that's what we really think it is."

On a typical day during the Megatransect, Fay and his team walked from 5:30 in the morning until 3:00 in the afternoon. The Pygmies then set up camp while Fay spent several hours downloading GPS data and repairing equipment. "By the time 10:30 or so rolled around, you'd die," Fay recalled. "People ask, 'What did you do to amuse yourself?' Are you kidding? Ain't no time." David Quammen, a *National Geographic* writer who accompanied Fay on several sections of the walk, noted that "On the trail he's good company, a man of humor and generous intellect. He sets a punishing pace, starting at daylight, never stopping to lunch or rest, but when there are field data to record in his yellow notebook, fortunately, he pauses often."

In fact, Fay stopped to examine and record the contents of every pile of animal droppings he saw along the way. He also measured every major tree he passed and noted every animal he encountered. Fay shared his observations along the Megatransect in a series of 75 field dispatches that appeared on the National Geographic Society Web site. "We're having a

Fay's epic walk through Africa took him into murky swamps such as this one in the Goualougo region.

great time," he wrote in one dispatch. "Been out on the trail for eight weeks now, walking through the mud, chopping our way through the rough patches. The forest is keeping us busy with elephants, gorillas, chimpanzees, monkeys, monitor lizards, aardvarks, hinge tortoises, and tons of other wildlife. We've arrived in a place called Goualougo, which is one of the deeper parts of the Ndoki Forest. We've dubbed it the Last Place on Earth because that's what we really think it is."

Fay and his team endured many hardships during the Megatransect. For example, they fought a constant battle against jungle pests like tsetse flies, stinging ants, leeches, and foot worms. At one point, Fay's feet were infested with 32 worms. "Imagine an inchworm burrowing through your toe like it burrows through a stringbean, except a much smaller version, and imagine how much that would itch. I had a bunch of those crawling along, gnawing at my flesh," he recalled. "It's a balance between the physical and the supernatural, really. If you can keep from being bothered by your physical body and just walk through the forest, then you can enjoy it. But if you're conscious of having bugs all over you and that you're hot and sweating, then you're not going to be able to appreciate the forest." Fay eventually began wrapping his feet in duct tape to protect them from the worms.

The team faced a number of potentially dangerous animals along their route, including poisonous snakes, hungry crocodiles, charging elephants, and angry gorillas. They also braved the hidden dangers of such tropical diseases as malaria, hepatitis, and Ebola virus. In May 2000, one of Fay's Pygmy porters, Mouko, became so ill with hepatitis that he had to be evacuated. Fay deviated from his route in order to deliver Mouko to a village at the edge of the forest. This detour forced Fay to miss walking an 18-mile section of the Megatransect, which he later referred to as the Mouko Gap.

Perhaps the most difficult struggles faced by Fay and his team were against the jungle itself. Fay's decision to walk through the center of the forest corridor, remaining as far as possible from human settlements, forced them to travel over mountains and through swamps. "We crossed a doozy of a swamp today, without a doubt the most unpleasant swamp we've crossed since the beginning of the trip," Fay wrote in January 2000. "It's very slow going. It's excruciatingly slow. And once in a while, you're up to your knee at best and up to your deep thigh at worst in this muck, you know, like chocolate pudding. You pull your leg out and it just kind of oozes up and leaves about a centimeter of a thick coat of this goo on your leg. And you carry on."

In one section of dense jungle, known as the Green Abyss, the team had to use a machete to whack a tunnel through a sea of green stems 15 feet high. Their forward progress was limited to 60 steps per hour, and they managed to walk less than a mile during one 10-hour day. Despite all the hardships, though, Fay remained committed to his goals throughout the journey. "I literally want as many people on Earth as possible to see this place and to fall in love with it. And to help," he stated. "That's what I want, and everything we're doing out here is for that reason."

Completing the Megatransect

Fay completed the Megatransect on December 18, 2000, when he reached the Atlantic Coast of Gabon after spending 456 days walking through the jungle. He emerged from the forest on a pristine beach that was teeming with wildlife, including hippos body-surfing in the waves. None of the Pygmies accompanying him had ever seen the ocean before. In fact, they were frightened of the surf because they had heard legends about a salty river with no end that was inhabited by sorcerers. Fay remembered convincing one of his porters to approach the sea: "We hit the coastal scrub and Bebe stopped. It was only 100 meters to the coast. He was afraid. I coaxed him along, and he continued, now decided. We broke out onto a treeless, green buffalo pasture. It went down a gentle slope to the beach. It was beautiful, just as I remembered. I had big tears in my eyes. I was overwhelmed. Suddenly the walk was over. . . . We sat on the beach for a while, and I called my parents."

Although Fay was pleased to have succeeded, he also found it difficult to accept that his journey was over. "When I got out of the forest and reached the Gabonese coast, it was three days before I would even think about putting on a shirt. I wasn't jonesing for anything. I just wanted to stay out there, to keep going. I didn't want to shower or drink a cold beer or eat a hamburger," he noted. "We had come so far, for so long. It had become a way of life. I would gladly have turned back and done it all again."

Fay collected a monumental amount of scientific data during the Megatransect. He returned to civilization with dozens of notebooks full of observations, 300 hours of video, 100 hours of audio, and 2,400 rolls of film. He counted 40,000 piles of animal droppings, measured 35,000 trees, and suffered 5,000 fly bites over the course of his journey. Although his team rarely went hungry for more than a day or two between airdrop resupplies, Fay still lost 40 pounds from the physical exertion. "My body looks like a marathoner now," he said. "My upper torso has diminished down into nothingness and my legs look like Mr. Atlas."

"We crossed a doozy of a swamp today, without a doubt the most unpleasant swamp we've crossed since the beginning of the trip," Fay reported. "It's excruciatingly slow. And once in a while, you're up to your knee at best and up to your deep thigh at worst in this muck, you know, like chocolate pudding."

In early 2001, Fay flew to the United States to set up a computer database for his Megatransect research. He also shared his experiences in numerous interviews in an attempt to drum up support for his conservation work. "The biggest realization for me on this Megatransect is the fact that there are still several places in central Africa . . . that are very special," he stated. "These are places that are completely pristine and functioning ecosystems. Everything is there. It all makes sense and as soon as there's any kind of disturbance, it starts to fall apart. It doesn't make sense anymore. And I think that we have a responsibility to identify these places, take a good look at them."

Fay's epic journey was covered in a three-part series of articles in *National Geographic* magazine, which appeared in the October 2000, March 2001, and August 2001 issues. The Megatransect was also featured in an hour-long *National Geographic Explorer* television program called "Africa Extreme." Fay used the publicity surrounding the Megatransect to draw worldwide attention to the need to preserve the Congo Basin rainforest. "My life will never be the same," he explained. "I am now completely comfortable in the forest, like I belong here, like I've always been here. It is a place that is alive and abundant when it is left to grow. I think about protecting it now every day, much of the day, and risk being taken like some religious fanatic preaching about the forest, trying somehow to convince others to see the light."

"My life will never be the same,"Fay declared. "I am now completely comfortable in the forest, like I belong here, like I've always been here. It is a place that is alive and abundant when it is left to grow. I think about protecting it now every day, much of the day, and risk being taken like some religious fanatic preaching about the forest, trying somehow to convince others to see the light."

Winning Protection for 13 New Parks in Gabon

After completing the Megatransect, Fay presented his message about the need to protect African forests to U.S. and world leaders. The main focus of his conservation efforts was Gabon, the country where he completed the Megatransect. Gabon is located at the Equator in west-central Africa. At 103,000 square miles, it is about the same size as the state of Colorado. Over 80 percent of its land area is covered by tropical forest, although much of this forest is threatened by logging. Gabon is one of the few countries in the region with a stable government, which has been led for 30 years by President El Hadj Omar Bongo. With 1.2 million people, it is also one of the least densely populated countries in Africa. The combination of all these factors led Fay to view Gabon as a prime candidate to create a national park system to preserve his beloved rainforest.

In 2002, Fay met with President Bongo of Gabon and encouraged him to protect his country's natural resources. "I started showing him pictures [on a laptop computer screen] taken by my friend at the National Geographic

Fay warily films an approaching elephant.

Society, Nick Nichols, who was my partner on the Megatransect," Fay related. "[Nick's photos captured] surfing hippos, gorillas in clearings, elephants in the forest, and gorillas and chimpanzees caressing their young. The president was transported into the computer. He was there. You could see right away that he was blown away by what he saw. He kept asking his foreign minister, 'How come I don't know about these things? We must act quickly.' He said, 'We're going to do something dramatic. We need to develop tourism in our country. We need to shift the economy to a more diversified one. These are unbelievable resources in our country that we haven't thought about.'"

Fay initially hoped to convince President Bongo to establish one national park to preserve Langoue Bai, a rare, mineral-rich clearing in the forest where elephants and other animals gather. But the leader of Gabon was so impressed by the results of Fay's work that he went further than Fay ever dreamed possible. On August 30, 2002, President Bongo signed a series of decrees that created a network of 13 national parks covering 10,000 square miles, or nearly 11 percent of Gabon's total land area. "By creating these national parks, we will develop a viable alternative to simple exploitation of natural resources that will promote the preservation of our environment," Bongo explained. "Gabon has the potential to become a natural Mecca, attracting pilgrims from the four points of the compass in search of the last remaining natural wonders on earth." Experts called the

65

The data Fay gathered during his Megatransect convinced Gabonese President El Hadj Omar Bongo to protect nearly 10,000 square miles of wilderness.

president's dramatic move one of the most significant conservation actions in history. "With the president's decision," Quammen wrote in *National Geographic,* "Gabon has pledged to become one of the world's leading stewards of biological diversity."

Fay understood that the government of Gabon did not possess the financial resources to manage such a large park system, so he began working to secure international aid. He met with members of the U.S. Congress, and he led Secretary of State Colin Powell on a tour of the beach in Gabon where he completed the Megatransect. Thanks in part to his efforts, the U.S. government contributed $53 million to the Congo Basin Forest Partnership, an international effort to support natural resource management in Gabon and other countries in the region. The money will be used to help Gabon develop infrastructure for the parks, create training programs for employees, enforce rules and boundaries, and attract tourists.

"The grand plan is for Gabon to become the Costa Rica of the East," Fay said, referring to the popular ecotourism destination in the rainforests of Central America. "The world should regard Gabon as the natural paradise of tropical forest Africa. We want people to think about Gabon as a place to see an unbelievable abundance of nature." Fay hoped that Gabon's decision would encourage neighboring countries to create new national parks. "I think that this wave we've begun will translate into significant conservation action in every country in central Africa," he stated. "President Bongo can lead the way. He's a very well-respected, regal man. People listen to him."

Dedicating His Life to Saving Wild Places

Fay continues to work as a field researcher for the Wildlife Conservation Society. He is also employed as a conservation fellow by the National Geographic Society. Although he is trained as a scientist, Fay views himself as a conservationist. He claims that his main job is to raise public awareness of the unique forest ecosystems in Africa and lead efforts to protect the remaining forests from destruction. "What I am trying to show the world, in a desperate way, is that we're just about to lose the last little gems on the African continent," he stated. "If we don't do something now — today — we can forget about it."

By any measure, Fay has been remarkably successful in his conservation efforts. Fay "has done more than anyone else to bring attention to the stakes we all have in conserving the Congo Basin forests," said Ed Royce, U.S. congressman from California and chairman of the House International Relations Committee Subcommittee on Africa. "Especially for young people, . . . Michael Fay is a testament to the great difference in the world that one determined person can make."

Fay has maintained his enthusiasm despite a recent close encounter with wildlife. In February 2003 he was leading a group of scientists through Loango National Park in Gabon when he was attacked by an elephant. The other members of his group fled while Fay stayed behind to fend off the charge. The elephant knocked him down and repeatedly tried to pin him to the ground with its tusks, but Fay was able to grab the tusks and guide them away from his body. The elephant stopped the attack only after a member of his group returned and threw a backpack at it. Fay suffered numerous cuts and bruises on his arms and legs, including a puncture of his right biceps, but escaped serious injury. "I feel like the luckiest person on the planet," he said afterward. "All I could see were those tusks bearing down on my chest, and I thought that it was a miracle that I hadn't been killed."

Fay did not let the incident distract him from his mission. In fact, he is currently planning a three-year transect of all of Africa. "My approach starts from my love of wild places and wild things," he explained. "To be out there looking at the natural world and living in it, is a dream come true. It's the way I want to live. The hardship of it is not really even a question. If you have that kind of mindset, then ultimately, you are compelled to do as much as you can to preserve the last remaining wild places."

Despite his many successes, Fay remains deeply concerned about the future of Africa's forests, as well as the larger environment. He places blame for the crisis squarely on shortsighted policies that lead to overconsumption of the world's resources. "Human beings, even in the 21st century, still don't regard natural resources as something precious. Because if they did, there would be a worldwide effort to preserve these places rather than extract wood out of them as quickly as possible with zero regard for ecosystems," he declared. "We need to educate everyone on the planet that we still need Mother Nature to survive and that abundance is good. We are intelligent enough to figure out how we can save the majority of species on earth; we can assure that water continues to flow and plants continue to grow and wildlife survives. It is an attainable goal and one that we need to accomplish as fast as we possibly can."

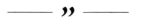

> "Human beings, even in the 21st century, still don't regard natural resources as something precious. Because if they did, there would be a worldwide effort to preserve these places rather than extract wood out of them as quickly as possible with zero regard for ecosystems."

MARRIAGE AND FAMILY

Michael Fay married Andrea Turkalo, an elephant researcher whom he met in the Peace Corps, in 1979. Due to the demands of their careers, Fay and his wife only see each other a few days each year. "We're still officially married," he noted. "Proximity is not part of the equation." Fay describes his marriage as "a very peculiar relationship, sometimes very difficult," but "still intense." "We have a bond that's very strong, which is this window into nature—and we both relate to that very well," he added.

One of Fay's employers, the National Geographic Society, maintains a small apartment for him in Washington, D.C. But since completing the Megatransect, Fay has had trouble accepting such modern conveniences as beds, toilets, and automobiles. In fact, he prefers to sleep in a tent in Washington's Rock Creek Park, go to the bathroom outdoors, and ride a bicycle around the city. Fay spends as little time in Washington as possible and considers the forests of Africa to be his home. "I will never live in the United States again except for short terms. There's nothing for me here, nothing to keep me here," he stated. "I've lost interest in everything but [conservation]. Material wealth has vanished off the radar screen for me.

Any thought of owning something or building something that is mine just isn't important to me."

HOBBIES AND OTHER INTERESTS

Fay claims that his commitment to conservation leaves no time for other pursuits. "Throughout my life, I've always been 100 percent focused on expanding my knowledge of the natural world and trying to do something about the fact that humans don't live sustainably on the planet," he declared. "I've never been distracted by any other interest." He admits to reading occasional books about American history, particularly the Vietnam War, during his treks through African jungles. Fay also possesses a strong ability to learn languages. He speaks English, French, Arabic, Sangho (the native language of the Central African Republic), Lingala (the native language of the Republic of Congo), and some Pygmy.

MAJOR INFLUENCES

Not surprisingly, Fay counts a fellow conservationist among his heroes. "Richard Leakey captivated millions around the globe to save elephants and African wildlife and brought huge resources to rebuild the park system in Kenya," he noted. "He works to reconcile the reality of human population with the desire to preserve ecosystems and is a hard-working, brave, and honorable human being."

SELECTED WRITINGS

"Logging, Forest Ecosystems, and People in Northern Congo," Congressional Testimony, U.S. House of Representatives International Relations Committee, Subcommittee on Africa, Mar. 19, 1997
"Walk for Wildlife: A Quest to Save One of Africa's Most Spectacular Wild Places," *Wildlife Conservation,* Sep./Oct. 2001, p.36
"Saving the Congo Basin," Congressional Testimony, U.S. House of Representatives International Relations Committee, Subcommittee on Africa, Mar. 11, 2003

FURTHER READING

Periodicals

Current Biography Yearbook, 2001
GeoWorld, Sep. 2001, p.46
Harper's, July 2002, p.41

Independent (London), Sep. 21, 2001, p.8
National Geographic, Oct. 2000, p.2; Mar. 2001, p.2; Aug. 2001, p.75; Apr.
   2003, p.90; Sep. 2003, p.50
National Geographic Adventure, July/Aug. 2001, p.80; Sep. 2003, p.38
National Geographic World, Sep. 2001, p.26
New York Times, Feb. 9, 2003, p.41
New Yorker, May 14, 2001, p.50
Newark (NJ) Star-Ledger, Apr. 6, 2001, p.63
St. Louis Post-Dispatch, Mar. 14, 1989, p.D1; Oct. 23, 1991, p.F1
Science, Aug. 6, 1999, p.825
Time, July 13, 1992, p.62
USA Today, Sep. 4, 2002, p.D8
U.S. News and World Report, Aug. 20, 2001, p.60
Washington Post, Mar. 17, 2001, p.C1
Wildlife Conservation, Sep./Oct. 2001, p.36

Online Articles

http://www.esri.com/news/arcnews/
   (*ArcNews Online,* "Dr. Michael Fay, the Man out of Africa," Fall 2001)
http://news.nationalgeographic.com/news/
   (*National Geographic News,* "Interview: Mike Fay Is on a Trek to Preserve
   Forest in Gabon," Aug. 9, 2001; "Africa Explorer Plans More Epic Treks
   to Save Wilds," Dec. 20, 2002)
http://www.pbs.org/wnet/religionandethics/
   (*Religion and Ethics Newsweekly,* "Feature: J. Michael Fay," Aug. 31, 2001)
http://www.twp.org/wildearth/
   (*Wild Earth Journal,* "Interview: Mike Fay," Fall 2002)

ADDRESS

Michael Fay
Wildlife Conservation Society
2300 Southern Blvd.
Bronx, NY 10460

WORLD WIDE WEB SITES

http://www.nationalgeographic.com/congotrek
http://wcs.org
http://www.savethecongo.org
http://www.savingwildplaces.com

Laura L. Kiessling 1960-
American Chemist and Professor
Conducted Groundbreaking Research into the Causes
of Alzheimer's Disease and the Inflammation of Body
Tissue

BIRTH

Laura Lee Kiessling (pronounced KIZ-ling) was born September 21, 1960, in Milwaukee, Wisconsin. She is the daughter of William E. Kiessling, a lawyer, and LaVonne "Bonnie" V. (Korth) Kiessling. She has two younger brothers, William III and Mark.

YOUTH

Laura grew up in Lake Mills, Wisconsin. Although no one in her family was a scientist, she always showed natural curiosity and interest in the world around her. Her brother Bill remembered a story their mother often told to demonstrate Laura's early powers of observation. When Laura was about three years old, she watched intently as her mother changed Bill's diaper. Realizing that Laura was contemplating the differences between boys and girls, "Mom asked, 'Laura, is there anything you'd like to ask me?'" Bill recalled. "Laura said, 'No, I got it figured out.' 'Really, what's that?' Mom asked. And Laura said, 'Boys have outdoor plumbing, and girls have indoor plumbing.'"

>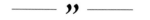
>
> *Kiessling loved to conduct scientific experiments as a child. "One time I tried to put little motors on the end of a Frisbee that would fire in opposite directions to make it spin really fast,"* she recalled.

As she grew older, Laura enjoyed doing scientific experiments. She and her brother Bill received a science kit that included materials and instructions for some basic experiments, like making a lie detector and other gadgets. Once they had tried all of the experiments that were included in the kit, they started creating their own. "We rigged it up to give a small shock to the doorknob and then tricked our younger brother Mark into opening the door," Laura related. Of course, not all of her childhood experiments were successful. "One time I tried to put little motors on the end of a Frisbee that would fire in opposite directions to make it spin really fast," she remembered. Unfortunately, the Frisbee was too heavy to fly and ended up sputtering on the lawn. "I forgot about the idea of buoyancy," she acknowledged. "Let's just say it wasn't very aerodynamic."

EDUCATION

Kiessling was a good student throughout her school years in Lake Mills. Upon graduating from high school, she started taking classes at the University of Wisconsin in Madison. After completing her first semester, however, she transferred to the Massachusetts Institute of Technology (MIT) in Cambridge. She majored in chemistry and also acted as captain of the women's crew team at MIT. She often got up at 4:30 in the morning to attend rowing practice before going to the lab.

Kiessling earned a bachelor of science degree in chemistry from MIT in 1983. She went on to pursue doctoral studies at Yale University in New Haven, Connecticut. She served as a teaching assistant and laboratory research assistant during her time at Yale. After earning her Ph.D. in chemistry in 1989, she accepted a position as a postdoctoral research fellow at the California Institute of Technology (Cal Tech).

CAREER HIGHLIGHTS

In 1991 Kiessling returned to her home state and joined the faculty of the University of Wisconsin, which enjoys a strong reputation in the fields of science and engineering. Kiessling started out as an assistant professor of chemistry. She was promoted to associate professor in 1997. Two years later she was named a full professor of chemistry and biochemistry—a position she continues to hold.

Kiessling's research at the university focuses on synthetic chemistry. She designs and creates artificial molecules that can change the action of natural compounds in the body and thus shed light on processes related to disease. One of her main areas of interest involves the sticky molecules that coat most cells in the body and allow them to adhere selectively to other cells. Cell adhesion, or stickiness, is key to a variety of biological processes, including bacterial infection, inflammation, and fertilization.

Over the years, Kiessling has earned a national reputation as one of the top scientists in her field. "Kiessling stands out among organic chemists because of her remarkable and original research program," a colleague told *Chemical and Engineering News*. "She has identified problems that both chemists and biologists find to be exceedingly important, and she is elucidating [defining] these problems with insightful experimental approaches that employ a wide variety of methods."

Finding a New Way to Combat Inflammation

Kiessling's early research work focused on ways to fight inflammation of body tissues. Inflammation is a natural immune system response to injury or disease. The outward signs of inflammation include redness, swelling, heat, and pain in the affected area. It occurs when white blood cells leave the bloodstream and enter the tissues surrounding an injury. "Say you smash your finger and it swells up," Kiessling said. "That's because white blood cells have been recruited to that area."

White blood cells are guided through the bloodstream by carbohydrate-coated molecules called L-selectins. When the body signals that white

Kiessling talks in her research laboratory with one of her graduate students.

blood cells are needed to respond to an injury, the cells move toward the walls of the blood vessels carrying them. The L-selectin molecules adhere to the walls, which are covered with sticky binding proteins. The chemical reaction opens a "door" in the wall of the blood vessel for the white blood cells to pass through. "The many copies of L-selectin on the white blood cell surface bind with the many copies of the L-selectin binding protein on the blood vessel, much like fingers fitting into a glove," Kiessling explained. "The inflammatory response depends on the cells sticking together."

Since inflammation is a natural immune system response, it is usually associated with the healing process. But inflammation can cause discomfort and, in some situations, even endanger a patient's health. For example, some people's immune systems become overactive and attack their joints or tissues, leading to diseases like arthritis, lupus, and multiple sclerosis. Inflammation may also be dangerous for people with cancer. "Cancer cells have a similar carbohydrate to those occurring on white blood cells," Kiessling noted. "People think cancer cells might metastasize [spread] to new sites using the normal pathways a white blood cell might go through."

Efforts to combat inflammation have developed into a multi-billion dollar industry. But common treatments — which include ice packs and pain relievers like aspirin and ibuprofen — only take effect after the white blood cells have already left the bloodstream. This means the treatments do not help people with autoimmune diseases or cancer. Kiessling wanted to find a way to prevent inflammation from occurring in the first place. Her research centered on the adhesion of L-selectin molecules with blood vessel walls, which was key to the inflammation process. "We're really trying to figure out what's going on at the molecular level," she stated. "What's important are the forces that hold these things together."

Kiessling spent many years trying to create a synthetic carbohydrate that would stick to the blood vessel walls in place of L-selectins. She hoped that these molecules would block white blood cells from leaving the bloodstream, thus stopping the process of inflammation. In 1998 she published her findings in the journal *Nature*. In her article, Kiessling announced that she had created synthetic sugar molecules called neoglycopolymers that effectively blocked white blood cells from leaving the bloodstream. Even more impressive, the neoglycopolymers snipped the binding proteins from the walls of blood vessels, thus preventing future inflammation. "It's like doing surgery on a really small part of the cell's surface," she noted. "We're removing a protein that facilitates [triggers] an unwanted inflammatory response. One advantage of this strategy is that it's not reversible, so cells no longer adhere."

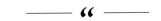

In 1998 Kiessling unveiled a process that helped stop tissue inflammation. "It's like doing surgery on a really small part of a cell's surface," she explained.

Other scientists praised Kiessling's work. Samuel Danishefsky of Columbia University called her approach "a genuinely new idea" and said that it had "massive implications." For example, it could help prevent the spread of diseased blood cells through the body, and it could lead to new classes of anti-inflammatory drugs. Stuart L. Schreiber of Harvard University, who was Kiessling's graduate adviser at Yale, added that her work "has opened up an exciting new area of research at the interface of organic chemistry and biology."

In 1999 Kiessling received a $285,000 fellowship from the MacArthur Foundation. Commonly known as "genius grants," MacArthur fellowships are granted to between 20 and 40 individuals each year in various fields, such as science, literature, music, teaching, and activism. In addition to past achievements, they recognize recipients' talent, creativity, and potential to make great contributions to society. Kiessling was allowed to use the money in whatever way she chose. "I want to think about it a while so I can do something that really makes a difference," she stated.

Discovering a Possible Treatment for Alzheimer's Disease

Even as she continued her inflammation prevention research, Kiessling turned her attention to another health problem. Working with Regina Murphy, a professor of chemical engineering at Wisconsin, she conducted studies on the causes of Alzheimer's disease. Alzheimer's disease affects two million Americans and kills more than 100,000 each year, making it the fourth-leading cause of death in the United States. Victims of this disease experience the systematic destruction of their brain cells. They suffer progressive disorientation, loss of memory and reasoning, and eventually death. There is no definitive treatment for the disease, and no known cure.

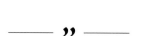

"If we can use our synthetic approach to understand how vaccines work and understand what makes a good vaccine and a bad vaccine, then we could direct vaccine development towards creating more effective vaccines that have fewer side effects."

One of the main characteristics of Alzheimer's disease is that the brain tissue of patients contains poisonous plaque deposits. These deposits are composed of sticky protein molecules called beta-amyloids. Beta-amyloid molecules are harmless until they clump together to form long fibrils. The fibrils harden into plaque, become toxic, and kill surrounding nerve cells in the brain. The density of the clumps tends to increase as the disease progresses, leading scientists to believe that the plaque deposits interfere with the normal functioning of the brain.

Kiessling and Murphy decided to find a way to disrupt the fibril-forming process. They created synthetic "inhibitor" protein molecules that would stick to beta-amyloids. The synthetic molecules essentially tricked the beta-amyloids into sticking to them instead of to other beta-amyloids. Rather than forming long fibrils, the inhibitor proteins and beta-amyloids formed tiny bundles that were nontoxic. The synthetic proteins also helped to break up existing fibrils. They worked on the same principle as household detergent, grabbing the clumps and forcing them to dissolve. "It's a really simple idea and, as far as we know, there are few strategies that target this step in the process," Kiessling noted.

In 1997 Kiessling and Murphy reported that they had found a way to disrupt the formation of plaque deposits in the brain associated with Alzheimer's disease. They hoped that their research might lead to the development of new drugs that could slow down or even stop the process that destroys the mental functions of Alzheimer's patients. "This is an exciting development," said John Cross, chief scientist at the American Health Assistance Foundation. "It has the possibility of interfering with the progression of Alzheimer's. If there is something that can prevent nerve cell death, perhaps we can stop the disease."

Shedding New Light on Bacterial Communication

In the late 1990s Kiessling launched a new avenue of research involving bacterial communication. All living cells, including bacteria, respond to chemical signals in their environment by grabbing them with surface receptors. The receptors are protein molecules that function like tiny noses or tongues. "The receptors act like a sensory organ and help the cell integrate and respond to many different signals," Kiessling noted.

For 30 years scientists thought that each chemical signal in a cell's environment interacted with one specific type of receptor. But Kiessling proved that bacteria cells use all four major types of surface receptors simultaneously to detect, retrieve, and process chemicals in their environment. "What we showed was it's not just one type of protein but this whole array of proteins on the cell surface," she explained. "All the proteins collaborate with each other."

Kiessling's experiments centered on the disease-causing bacteria Escherichia coli. Commonly known as E. coli, it is found in the feces of humans and many animals. E. coli has 5,000 surface receptors and can detect changes as small as 5 percent in the concentration of substances in its environment. These chemical signals help E. coli decide how and where to move, and whether or not to grow and multiply. E. coli uses its tail-like flagella to swim toward nutrients and avoid potentially damaging chemicals.

Working with graduate student Jason Gestwicki, Kiessling developed synthetic protein molecules called ligands that interacted with E. coli's arrays of receptor molecules and influenced the movement of the bacteria. They described their findings in a 2002 article for *Nature*. "What we've done for the first time is show that you can use a synthetic ligand to systematically control a cellular response," Kiessling stated.

Although Kiessling's research focused on a specific bacteria, her most important finding—that surface receptors work together to process information—should apply to many types of cells. Some fellow scientists believe that she may have discovered the "Achilles heel," or hidden weakness, of bacteria. The results of her experiments could help researchers design

Kiessling's work in the laboratory has led to new developments in research into tissue inflammation, Alzheimer's disease, and disease-causing bacteria.

compounds that interfere with the bacterial signaling process and thus protect people from disease. For example, they could lead to the development of chemicals that repel germs from surfaces in schools and hospitals. They could also facilitate the creation of better vaccines. "If we can use our synthetic approach to understand how vaccines work and understand what makes a good vaccine and a bad vaccine, then we could direct vaccine development towards creating more effective vaccines that have fewer side effects," Kiessling explained.

Combining Research and Teaching

When asked to name a trait that distinguishes Kiessling from other scientists, her students and colleagues mention her intellectual fearlessness. Throughout her career, Kiessling has demonstrated a willingness to step outside of her areas of expertise and try new things. Although she was trained as a chemist, she looks for opportunities to apply her research to real-life problems in the field of biology. Her willingness to "think outside the box" has enabled her to find innovative new approaches to old problems. "Laura has a passion for research," stated colleague Peter B. Dervan, who worked with Kiessling at Cal Tech. "Her fire and enthusiasm inspire all who are around her. In addition, she has the courage to take risks and is willing to work on complicated research problems."

Kiessling's groundbreaking research has earned her a number of prestigious awards and fellowships, as well as membership in several highly regarded professional organizations. In 2002, for example, Kiessling was elected to the American Association for the Advancement of Science. The following year she was elected to the American Academy of Arts and Scientists, a learned organization that provides a forum for members to become involved in projects that serve the needs of society.

Kiessling has received several patents for her work over the years. In 2000 she and her husband formed a biotechnology company, called Quintessence Biosciences, to develop and market products based on their scientific research. The company is located near Madison, Wisconsin. Its name comes from an ancient word for the fifth element of matter, which is the underlying essence or spirit of a substance (the other four elements are earth, water, fire, and air).

In addition to her contributions to scientific research, Kiessling is known as an outstanding teacher at the University of Wisconsin. She creates an intellectually stimulating environment in her lab that encourages creativity and independence in her stu-

———— " ————

"Many people don't know what it's like to be an academic scientist—how flexible and multifaceted your job is. You never know for sure what you'll end up doing that day," Keissling said. "I worry that we discourage young, talented, creative people from going into chemistry because it sounds like you have to give up everything and just think about chemistry."

———— " ————

dents. Kiessling disputes the notion that chemistry is a solitary pursuit that requires scientists to spend all their time in the lab. "Many people don't know what it's like to be an academic scientist—how flexible and multifaceted your job is. You never know for sure what you'll end up doing that day," she noted. "I worry that we discourage young, talented, creative people from going into chemistry because it sounds like you have to give up everything and just think about chemistry." Asked to describe the most satisfying aspects of her job, Kiessling replied: "Interactions with students and other scientists, talking about science, finding out something new, and talking about what's the next great experiment that we can do."

———— " ————

Although initially hesitant about having a child, Kiessling says that the transition to parenthood has been easy for her. "Having a child changed my life much less than I thought it would," she noted. "It has been easier for me because I have a supportive spouse."

———— " ————

MARRIAGE AND FAMILY

Kiessling is married to Ronald T. Raines, a professor of biochemistry at the University of Wisconsin at Madison. Her husband's research focuses on the use of proteins in fighting diseases like cancer. The couple has a daughter, Kyra, who was born in 1998. They came up with her name, which means "shining light," by combining the first syllables of their last names (Kie-Ra).

Kiessling was initially hesitant about having a child, but her husband eventually talked her into it. "Laura was worried that if we had a kid and things behaved in the traditional way, then it would be detrimental to her career, which is extremely important to her," Raines recalled. "It took a while to reassure her that I would do 50 percent of the work, and finally she believed me." Kiessling says that the transition to parenthood has been easy for her. "Having a child changed my life much less than I thought it would," she noted. "It has been easier for me because I have a supportive spouse."

HOBBIES AND OTHER INTERESTS

In her spare time, Kiessling enjoys canoeing, rowing, and running.

SELECTED WRITINGS

"Synthetic Ligands Point to Cell Surface Strategies," *Nature,* Mar. 1, 1998 (with E.J. Gordon and W.J. Sanders)
"The Periodic Table of Biology," *Chemical and Engineering News,* Mar. 26, 2001
"Inter-receptor Communication through Arrays of Bacterial Chemoreceptors," *Nature,* Jan. 3, 2002 (with Jason E. Gestwicki)

HONORS AND AWARDS

Shaw Scientist Award (Milwaukee Foundation): 1992-97
National Young Investigator Award (National Science Foundation): 1993-98

Beckman Young Investigator Award: 1994-96
Zeneca Excellence in Chemistry Award: 1996
Camille Dreyfus Teacher-Scholar Award (Dreyfus Foundation): 1996
Sloan Fellowship (Alfred P. Sloan Foundation): 1997
MacArthur Fellowship (John D. and Catherine T. MacArthur Foundation): 1999
Arthur C. Cope Scholar Award (American Chemical Society): 1999
Isbell Award (American Chemical Society): 2000
Award for Creativity in Carbohydrate Chemistry (*Carbohydrate Research*): 2001
Romnes Fellowship: 2002
American Association for the Advancement of Science: 2002
American Academy of Arts and Sciences: 2003

FURTHER READING

Books

Who's Who in America, 2003
Who's Who in Science and Engineering, 2003

Periodicals

Chemical and Engineering News, Feb. 8, 1999, p.47; Jan. 31, 2000, p.25; Mar. 26, 2001
Current Biography Yearbook, 2003
Findings, Feb. 2001, p.9
Madison (WI) Capital Times, Feb. 6, 1999, p.A1; June 23, 1999, p.A1
Milwaukee Journal Sentinel, Jan. 3, 2002, p.1
Wisconsin State Journal, May 31, 1993, p.C1; Jan. 12, 1997, p.A1; Mar. 8, 1998, p.E1

Online Articles

http://www.madison.com
(*Wisconsin State Journal,* "UW Researcher Looks for Ways to Manipulate Carbohydrates," May 31, 1993)
http://www.news.wisc.edu
(*News@UW-Madison,* "Disarming Alzheimer's Toxic Proteins," Apr. 14, 1997; "Snipping Inflammation in the Bud," Mar. 1, 1998; "Study Suggests Way to Short-Circuit Microbe Communication," Jan 2. 2002)

http://www.wistechnology.com/QuintessenceSecuresFinancing.php
(*Wisconsin Technology Network,* "Quintessence Secures Financing,"
May 28, 2003)

ADDRESS

Professor Laura L. Kiessling
University of Wisconsin
Department of Chemistry
1101 University Avenue
Madison, WI 53706-1396

E-mail: kiessling@chem.wisc.edu

WORLD WIDE WEB SITES

http://www.chem.wisc.edu/
http://www.cmb.wisc.edu/

Alvin Poussaint 1934-
American Psychiatrist, Educator, and Activist
Expert on African-American Psychological Issues

BIRTH

Alvin Francis Poussaint was born on May 15, 1934, in East Harlem, a neighborhood in New York City. He was the seventh of eight children born to his parents, who were descended from Haitian immigrants. Poussaint had three sisters and four brothers. His father, Christopher Thomas Poussaint, at one time owned a print shop in East Harlem. He also worked at other jobs in the printing profession, including as a linotypist and typographer. His mother, Harriet Johnston Poussaint, stayed at home and cared for her large family.

YOUTH

Poussaint grew up in a strong, traditional Roman Catholic family. His father was attentive but emotionally reserved. Though he and his father were not close, Poussaint recalled that "I always knew that he supported me, particularly in education." His mother, meanwhile, was a constant source of love and support. Her presence, he said, "gave me a certain security while I was growing up."

Poussaint was a smart and curious child, but his love for learning grew especially strong after he came down with rheumatic fever when he was nine years old. Rheumatic fever is a disease that includes high fever, severe swelling and pain in the joints, and even inflammation of the heart. The disease confined him to a hospital for six months and kept him bedridden at home for months after that. Poussaint turned to books as his main source of entertainment during this time, and family members brought him a steady supply to read. In addition, he taught himself to play several musical instruments. This experience marked the beginning of his lifelong quest for knowledge.

> **"[My brother's drug addiction] motivated me to achieve something,"** Poussaint recalled. **"I visited him in drug wards. They are decrepit, depressing places. I kept telling myself, 'This cannot happen to me.'"**

Poussaint grew up surrounded by siblings, family, and friends, but not all of his early influences were positive. Crime and drug abuse were major problems in his neighborhood. "I saw addicts shoot up and vomit," he recalled. "I saw blood run right out of their arms. Sometimes one of them would shoot up and fall flat on his face. I was 12 years old when I started seeing this on the street." Around this time, one of his brothers became addicted to the powerful drug heroin. Seeing the difficulties that his brother went through had a big impact on Poussaint. "His situation motivated me to achieve something," he explained. "I thought that if I didn't, the same thing would happen to me. I visited him in drug wards. They are decrepit, depressing places. I kept telling myself: 'This cannot happen to me.'"

Poussaint avoided such troubles by studying hard during the school year. He also regularly attended a summer camp in upstate New York. His enrollment in the camp was arranged by his father, who was a member of the board of directors of a local YMCA. At camp, he was exposed to middle-class white youths who came from environments in which college degrees and professional careers were seen as high but attainable goals. "It opened up a whole new vista," said Poussaint. Unfortunately, Poussaint also was exposed to subtle and open forms of racism at the summer camp. He also had many unpleasant encounters with racist attitudes in high school. By his mid-teens, Poussaint had learned to brace himself for racist comments and discriminatory treatment whenever he ventured away from the mostly black neighborhoods of his youth.

EDUCATION

Education was extremely important to the Poussaint family. It was especially important to Poussaint's father, who recognized that education provided a clear path to success. As a result, Poussaint took his schoolwork seriously from an early age. "I was mischievous when I was in grade school," he remembered. "I talked in class. My conduct was not terrific, but my grades were. My mother told me I was intelligent. She nicknamed me 'The Brain.' She made me feel I had something special. Then it stuck. My friends started calling me 'The Brain,' too. I felt that I had something to live up to."

> *"My mother told me I was intelligent," said Poussaint. "She nicknamed me 'The Brain.' She made me feel I had something special. Then it stuck. My friends started calling me 'The Brain,' too. I felt that I had something to live up to."*

Poussaint became even more serious about school after his early bout with rheumatic fever. While in the hospital, he so admired the doctors who cared for him that he decided to become a doctor himself one day. From that point on he worked very hard on his studies, exhibiting particular talent in his science and math courses. In 1948 he passed a difficult citywide qualifying exam and was admitted into New York City's Peter Stuyvesant High School, a prestigious school for gifted students. Poussaint thrived at Stuyvesant High, where he was surrounded by bright, hard-working students. He became an editor with the school's literary magazine, won the school's creative writing award in his senior year, and played in the school band. Poussaint graduated in 1952.

Though Poussaint won admission to Yale University, his father urged him to stay closer to home. In 1952 he enrolled in New York's Columbia University, where he immersed himself in his pre-medical school studies. "I

As a young man, Poussaint's interests ranged from pursuing a medical career to fighting for civil rights.

was always studying," he said. "My time was fully devoted to activities around school."

Poussaint's concentration on academic studies was partly due to the social attitudes that dominated the campus, which was composed mostly of white students. Enrollment in the school was open to all races, but social life was in fact very segregated (divided according to race). Minority students received clear signals that the races shouldn't mix socially. There was a feeling among whites "that blacks shouldn't come to social events," recalled Poussaint. "They didn't expect you to show up at the dance."

Poussaint did establish friendships with some white classmates, but he was not invited to their homes because of racist parents. This experience — of being as capable as his fellow students yet excluded from most of the university's social events because of his race — made a powerful impression on Poussaint. He began to think deeply about how racism influenced the way African-Americans thought about themselves and their place in society.

In 1956 Poussaint earned his bachelor of arts degree at Columbia. He then prepared to go to medical school. Becoming a doctor requires lengthy training. After finishing the first four years of college, students must attend four years of medical school. At the end of medical school, the new doctors decide what field of medicine they want to practice. Then they complete a residency program of at least three years in that field.

Poussaint won a full scholarship in 1956 to the Cornell University Medical College in upstate New York. He was the only African-American in a class of 86 students. Over the next few years, Poussaint took much of his training at the same hospital in New York City where he had been born. Poussaint received his medical degree in 1960, but his training did not end there. From 1960 to 1964 he completed his residency at the University of California in Los Angeles (UCLA), where he studied psychiatry. Beginning as an intern, he soon became resident and chief resident at the Neuro-psychiatric Institute. He earned his medical degree in psychiatry in 1964.

CAREER HIGHLIGHTS

Poussaint's first job out of school combined his skills in medicine with his growing interest in racial issues. During the early 1960s he had closely watched the growth of the civil rights movement, a social movement aimed at securing equal rights for African-Americans. By the time he left UCLA in 1964, it had become a powerful source for social change in the United States. Around the time that Poussaint completed his schooling, he was contacted by Bob Moses, a former classmate at Stuyvesant High School. In the ensuing years, Moses had become the leader of the Student Nonviolent Coordinating Committee (SNCC), one of the nation's leading civil rights organizations. Moses asked Poussaint to come to Jackson, Mississippi, to head SNCC's Medical Committee for Human Rights. Poussaint accepted the position, eager to do his part to improve the lives of black Americans.

Poussaint headed the committee from 1964 to 1966. During these years, he led efforts to end racial segregation in health care facilities all across the segregated South. The committee also provided medical care to civil rights workers, whose peaceful demonstrations sometimes came under violent attack from white citizens and law enforcement officers.

In 1966 Poussaint left Mississippi to take a position as assistant professor of psychiatry at the Tufts University School of Medicine in Boston, Massachusetts. The position marked the start of a long career in academic institutions for Poussaint. In 1969 he moved from Tufts to the Harvard Medical School, also in Boston, where he served as an associate professor and later as professor of psychiatry. Poussaint also served for a time as dean of students at Harvard Medical School. He remains a member of the Harvard Medical School faculty today.

———— " ————

"All the segregation and discrimination was damaging their mental health more than anything else, and it was important to fight that," said Poussaint. "I understood that I had to be political and try to influence the larger society. I needed to learn how to write popular articles and get them places where I could reach black people, white people, the society."

———— " ————

When Poussaint began teaching at Harvard Medical School and treating clients in his private psychiatric practice, he made an important realization. "One of the most important ways I could help the mental health of black people was not one-on-one therapy," he recalled. "All the segregation and discrimination was damaging their mental health more than anything else, and it was important to fight that. I understood that I had to be political and try to influence the larger society. I needed to learn how to write popular articles and get them places where I could reach black people, white people, the society." It was this insight that led Poussaint to become one of the nation's leading experts on black psychological issues and an important spokesman for improving the living conditions of African-Americans.

Understanding the Impact of Racism

From the start of his career, Poussaint was deeply concerned with understanding the complex and contradictory emotions that hundreds of years of racism had created in African-Americans. He felt that white doctors and psychiatrists misunderstood the psychological needs and problems of black patients. White mental health professionals explained the problems of their black patients, and of black society as a whole, in terms of racial self-hatred. They said that blacks acted out because they despised their own condition. Beginning in the early 1970s, however, Poussaint challenged these ideas. Such theories, he charged, allow whites "to feel that

During the 1970s Poussaint became a recognized expert on American society and its impact on African-American families.

we [black people] are psychologically deranged, while they're posing as models of mental health." He pointed out that white racism was itself a form of mental illness. He also contended that black mental problems were a result of "repressed rage" at the mistreatment they received.

Poussaint knew about repressed rage from firsthand experience — particularly from his experiences while working in Mississippi in the mid-1960s. Leaving his office in Mississippi one day, Poussaint had been accosted by a white policeman who called out "Hey, boy! Come here." Poussaint asked the officer not to call him "boy," which drove the police officer into a rage. After frisking Poussaint, the officer demanded, "What's your name, boy?" "Dr. Poussaint," he replied. "I'm a physician." The officer demanded to know his first name and grew threatening when Poussaint hesitated. Finally, Poussaint told the officer his first name. "Alvin," the policeman bellowed, "the next time I call you, you come right away, you hear? You hear me, boy?" Profoundly humiliated by this public incident, Poussaint muttered, "Yes, sir."

The humiliation that he endured, Poussaint realized, was something that affected virtually all African-Americans. He believed that such experiences created psychological stress that could lead to withdrawal and depression, or to anger and violence. Over the next several years, Poussaint published his theories in prestigious academic journals. But he reached many more people through his writings in such mainstream periodicals as the *New York Times Magazine,* the popular black magazine *Ebony,* and the widely read women's magazine *Redbook.* On the strength of these articles, he gradually emerged as a leading spokesman for the African-American community on a wide range of social issues, from child rearing to suicide to motivation to grieving.

Poussaint also worked to make quality health care available to more African-Americans. Many African-Americans did not have access to high-quality health care, including mental health care. This problem was partly due to lack of investment in medical facilities in poor black neighborhoods. But Poussaint felt that the low number of black doctors and psychiatrists in the United States was another factor. In his experience, many African-Americans avoided seeking medical attention because they did not trust white doctors to provide them with proper care. With this in mind, Poussaint set out to increase the number of black doctors and psychiatrists in America. He used his membership in the American Psychiatric Association to organize a black caucus (action group) on the issue. He also lobbied the National Institute of Mental Health (NIMH) to pay special attention to the psychological issues facing minorities. His efforts led to the creation of a special unit at the NIMH to focus on such issues.

In 1975, Poussaint's 42-year-old brother Kenneth died after years of addiction to heroin and other drugs. "He died in an emergency room at Harlem Hospital," Poussaint said. "I had seen him put in a straitjacket at the state psychiatric hospital and incarcerated many times for petty crimes. He developed bacterial infections, and his body finally failed him. His death changed my life. I saw how profoundly self-destructive his behavior was. He was unable to see failure as a temporary setback." His brother's death further motivated Poussaint to improve the quality of mental health care for African-Americans.

Using the Written Word

Since 1972, Poussaint has published several important books that offer thoughtful, practical advice on dealing with the lingering effects of racism. His first book was a collection of his essays, titled *Why Blacks Kill Blacks* (1972). From 1970 to 1985 he wrote a weekly newspaper column called "Getting Along" that was syndicated in newspapers across the country. He has also provided introductions for several works written by comedian Bill Cosby, a close friend.

Poussaint's most famous book grew out of his work on issues concerning child rearing. Written with fellow psychiatrist James P. Comer, *Black Child Care* (1975) began with the assumption that racism and poverty created conditions for black children that were very different from those faced by white children. Using a question-and-answer format, the authors addressed many of the issues they had confronted over the years. The book was revised in 1993 and published as *Raising Black Children*. The book discusses a wide range of child-rearing topics, but Poussaint and Comer pay special attention to the need to curb violence among black children. "The way we raise our children *from the beginning*," they write, "and the way we teach them to handle anger, conflict, and frustration will help most." Reviewers praised the common-sense approach that the authors brought to the complex issues of raising children.

Poussaint cautions young black people not to ignore their depression or sadness. "It is not a moral weakness, and it doesn't mean you are less of a person because you reach out for help," he said.

In 2000, Poussaint published another important work on black health issues. Co-written with journalist Amy Alexander, *Lay My Burden Down: Unraveling Suicide and the Mental Health Crisis among African-Americans* sought to explain an alarming rise in suicide among African-Americans. Long thought to be a "white problem," suicide became more common among blacks beginning in 1980. The suicide rate among blacks doubled between 1980 and 1995, reaching eight deaths every year per 100,000 people. It thus became the third leading cause of death for black men between the ages of 15 and 24. Attempting to understand the reasons why suicide has become more common, Poussaint and Alexander point to widespread distrust of white mental health professionals by African-Americans as one factor. But they also suggest that depression and despair have become more common among disillusioned and impoverished black youth.

In *Lay My Burden Down*, Poussaint and Alexander both provide moving stories of the suicides that took the lives of family members. Poussaint considers his brother's death from drug use a slow form of suicide, and he and Alexander warn against a range of self-destructive behaviors, including drug use, gang involvement, and crime. Poussaint cautions young black people not to ignore their depression or sadness. "It is not a moral weakness, and it doesn't mean you are less of a person because you reach out for help," he stated.

Poussaint served as a consultant for "The Cosby Show," a popular family sitcom from 1984 to 1992.

The Conscience of "The Cosby Show"

Poussaint's public profile received another boost when he was hired as a consultant for "The Cosby Show," a half-hour situation comedy that ran on NBC-TV from 1984 to 1992 and continues to play in reruns on Nickelodeon. The show, created by and starring Bill Cosby as Cliff Huxtable, M.D., focused on the family life of the fictional Huxtable family. Unlike nearly every previous depiction of black families on TV, the Huxtables were a stable, well-adjusted, middle-class family with two working parents and children who planned to go on to college. The show quickly became one of the most popular programs on television, and it was widely hailed for changing the nation's perceptions of black families. Poussaint is given a great deal of credit for this change.

Cosby asked his old friend Poussaint to check the scripts for the show to make sure that medical issues were covered accurately. But Poussaint soon played a much more important role. He became the show's conscience, helping to screen out subtle stereotypes about race, gender, obesity, or age. He made suggestions that helped give more positive images of African-Americans, such as having people on the show read books by black authors and having Cosby wear sweatshirts from notable black universities and colleges, like Howard, Morehouse, and Tuskegee. Poussaint also consulted on the television series "A Different World" (1987-93), a spin-off of "The Cosby Show" that centered on life in an all-black college.

Poussaint's work on "The Cosby Show" helped make him one of the nation's most sought after consultants on African-American issues. He was especially in demand during the late 1980s and the early 1990s, when government agencies, private companies, and entertainment producers increased their efforts to review the racial climate of their organizations and programs. Poussaint remained politically active during this time as well. He served on the presidential campaigns of the Reverend Jesse Jackson in 1984 and Bill Clinton in 1992. He also consulted for the Congressional Black Caucus, a group of black lawmakers. In addition, he was a member of congressional delegations to Cuba and to the People's Republic of China, and he advised the U.S. Department of State, the Department of Health, Education, and Welfare, and the Federal Bureau of Investigation.

"Our challenge is to define creative ways in which media for children can be improved so they work not only to entertain, but to educate, instill values, and build positive attitudes," stated Poussaint. *"The reality is that raising a child is everyone's business."*

Poussaint also devoted a great deal of time and effort to community organizations. He served as a member of Action for Children's Television, advised the Boston University School of Social Work, and consulted with dozens of other agencies and companies. Through these and other activities, Poussaint remained closely engaged with the leaders and citizens of many African-American communities. "Dr. Poussaint is no ivory-tower psychiatrist," declared Jesse Jackson. "He is no armchair academician espousing theories and reaching conclusions from afar."

Using Media to Help Children

In 1994 Poussaint founded the Media Center at the Judge Baker Children's Center in Boston. The Media Center encourages collaboration between media artists, mental health professionals, and educators to use the media to promote healthy psychological development in children. "Our challenge is to define creative ways in which media for children can be improved so they work not only to entertain, but to educate, instill values, and build positive attitudes," stated Poussaint. "The reality is that raising a child is everyone's business."

The Media Center became the first mental health center ever to produce a national television pilot and series when it introduced "Willoughby's Wonders" in 1996. This live-action comedy/drama follows the adventures of a racially mixed soccer team in Boston's South End neighborhood. "It's a good story line . . . that engages children," explained Poussaint, "and we think children will watch and listen. Children's TV doesn't have to be filled with violence, car chases, and sexual innuendo to be entertaining." The show aired on a public television station in Boston, but it was not picked up and broadcast by any of the national TV networks.

Today, Poussaint remains one of the country's best-known experts on African-American psychological issues. Although he is nearing the age of retirement, he continues to write, teach at Harvard, consult with various organizations on issues affecting African-Americans, and direct operations at the Media Center. The birth of his daughter in 1999 has slowed his active pace, however. "I want to spend more time with my wife and family," he explained. "I've always liked the home stuff, children and the little pleasures that go along with that."

MARRIAGE AND FAMILY

Poussaint has been married two times, and he has a child from each marriage. His first marriage, in 1973, was to Ann Ashmore, a social worker. They had one son, Alan, and were divorced in 1988. In 1993 he married Tina Young, a doctor. In 1999 the couple had their first child, a daughter named Alison. Poussaint confessed that it was somewhat odd to become a father again at age 65. "I realize that you can't predict life," he said. "[I] just try to give her as much as possible. She has already contributed to my life, as I have contributed to hers." The family lives in the Boston area.

HOBBIES AND OTHER INTERESTS

As a younger man, Poussaint enjoyed active outdoor pursuits such as swimming, boating, and camping. As he became a nationally prominent consultant he devoted more and more of his time to charitable work and to serving on the boards of organizations. With the birth of his daughter in 1999, he cut back on activities outside the home and devoted himself once more to being an involved and caring father.

WRITINGS

Why Blacks Kill Blacks, 1972

Black Child Care: How to Bring Up a Healthy Black Child in America; A Guide to Emotional and Psychological Development, 1975 (with James P. Comer)

Raising Black Children: Two Leading Psychiatrists Confront the Educational, Social, and Emotional Problems Facing Black Children, 1992 (with James P. Comer)

Lay My Burden Down: Unraveling Suicide and the Mental Health Crisis among African-Americans, 2000 (with Amy Alexander)

HONORS AND AWARDS

Michael Schwerner Award: 1968

American Black Achievement Award in Business and the Professions (Johnson Publishing Company): 1986

John Jay Award for Distinguished Professional Achievement (Columbia University): 1987

Medgar Evers Medal of Honor (National Association for the Advancement of Colored People): 1988

FURTHER READING

Books

Contemporary Black Biography, 1993

Metcalf, George R. *Up from Within: Today's New Black Leaders,* 1971

Notable Black American Men, 1998

Notable Black American Scientists, 1998

Who's Who Among African-Americans, 2002

Who's Who in the World, 2003

Periodicals

American Medical News, Mar. 16, 1990, p.7

Boston-Bay State Banner, Nov. 2, 1995

Boston Globe, July 30, 1989, p.A11; July 19, 1996, p.G1

Boston Globe Magazine, Dec. 8, 1996, p.16

Chicago Tribune, Feb. 24, 1998, p.C17

Current Biography Yearbook, 1973

Dallas Morning News Sunday Reader, Feb. 18, 2001, p.J1

Ebony, June 2000, p.116

Newsweek, Jan. 25, 1993, p.55

Online Articles

http://www.bsi-international.com/interview_prt.htm
  (*BSI International,* "Exclusive Interview with Dr. Alvin Poussaint," 2002)
http://www.healthyplace.com/communities/depression/minorities_5.asp
  (*HealthyPlace.com Depression Community,* "Suicide Among Blacks," undated)

Online Databases

Biography Resource Center Online, 2003, articles from *Contemporary Authors Online,* 2001; *Contemporary Black Biography,* 1993; *Notable Black American Men,* 1998; *Notable Black American Scientists,* 1998; and *Who's Who Among African-Americans,* 2002

ADDRESS

Alvin Poussaint
The Media Center
Judge Baker Children's Center
3 Blackfan Circle
Boston, MA 02115

WORLD WIDE WEB SITES

http://www.hms.harvard.edu/orma/poussaint
http://www.jbcc.harvard.edu/media.htm

Sandra Steingraber 1959-

American Biologist, Ecologist, and Cancer Activist
Author of *Living Downstream: An Ecologist Looks at
Cancer and the Environment* and *Having Faith: An
Ecologist's Journey to Motherhood*

BIRTH

Sandra Kathryn Steingraber was born on August 27, 1959, in
Champaign, Illinois. She was adopted at a young age by Wil-
ber Francis Steingraber and Kathryn Marie (Maurer) Steingraber. Her adoptive mother worked as a biologist, and her
adoptive father was a teacher. She had one younger sister.

YOUTH

Steingraber grew up in the town of Pekin, Illinois, which is in the central part of the state. Many families in the region support themselves through farming, raising fields of corn, soybeans, and other crops. Pekin and the surrounding region is also home to a wide variety of factories and industrial facilities. As a result, Steingraber grew up in a community dominated by farmers and factory workers. In her book *Living Downstream*, she recalled that when she worked as a waitress, these men and women were her primary early morning customers. "A magical hour occurred between 4:00 and 5:00 a.m. when the last of the shift workers still occupied the booths and the first wave of farmers began lining up at the counter," she wrote. "Talk of union contracts mingled with discussions of weather and grain prices."

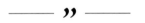

> "The scene I remember most vividly is unlocking my door and discovering that my roommate had moved out," Steingraber recalled. "She did not want to live with a cancer patient. Fifteen years later, the sight of a bare mattress can still cause me to burst into tears."

Though they brought jobs and prosperity, the farms and factories around Pekin also used large amounts of chemicals. Pesticides were sprayed on fields to control insects and weeds. Nearby factories, meanwhile, emitted chemicals into the community's air, earth, and water. By the time Steingraber reached adulthood, she realized that Pekin was "a very industrialized, very contaminated town."

Steingraber loved science from an early age. Some of her interest in science was inherited from her parents, especially her mother, Kathryn. "My mother was a biologist," Steingraber explained. "The first question I ever asked was 'how does the ear work?' I think I was born a biologist." Her interest in the subject of cancer also began with her mother. When Steingraber was 15 years old, her mother was diagnosed with breast cancer. Fortunately, she survived the disease, but the scare had a big influence on her daughter's choice of career. Up until that time, Steingraber had been interested in writing and literature in addition to science, and she had considered focusing on poetry or drama in college. After her mother became ill, however, she decided she would study biology as an undergraduate. She made this decision "because my mother was ill and maybe dying, and I wanted to carry her banner on."

Though her mother won her battle with cancer, the disease remained a familiar, frightening part of Steingraber's life. Her sister's fiancé died from colon cancer. Her aunt died from bladder cancer. Several uncles had other forms of the disease. "Cancer really shadowed my family for a while," Steingraber said.

Battling Cancer

But Steingraber's most intimate encounter with the disease took place when she herself was afflicted with bladder cancer. She was 20 years old at the time, attending college at Illinois Wesleyan University. Her treatment and recovery became a major part of her life between the ages of 20 and 25. She was able to survive the disease, but the procedures seemed endless and made other parts of her life difficult. "I kept my head down for those five years while I was going back in the hospital every three month for biopsies and cytoscopes [cancer tests and treatments]," she said. "I tried to live out my life in three-month segments between my checkups."

Steingraber's long cancer battle took a toll on some of her personal relationships as well. In *Living Downstream,* she recalls how one of her friends severed their relationship rather than confront the reality of the disease. "The scene I happen to remember most vividly — and this must have occurred weeks after my discharge from the hospital — is unlocking my door and discovering that my roommate had moved out," she said. "She did not want to live with a cancer patient. This was my redefining moment. Fifteen years later, the sight of a bare mattress can still cause me to burst into tears."

Steingraber's health gradually improved after years of treatment. But while she was grateful, she knew that the cancer might later reappear, a phenomenon known as recurrence. "Bladder cancer, like so many other cancers, is the kind of cancer that can come back years or even decades later," she explained. "I have never declared myself cured. On the other hand, I don't live my life waiting for the other shoe to drop."

EDUCATION

Steingraber attended public school in the Pekin school system, where she earned her high school diploma. She then continued her education at Illinois Wesleyan University in Bloomington. Despite battling cancer and enduring seemingly endless tests and treatments, she earned a bachelor of science degree from Illinois Wesleyan in 1981. During her years at the school, however, Steingraber also devoted a lot of time and energy to literature. In fact, she found that writing poetry about her experiences as a cancer patient helped her to come to terms with the disease.

After receiving her undergraduate degree, Steingraber decided to pursue her blossoming interest in writing and literature. She gained admission to the graduate creative writing program at Illinois State University in Normal, where she worked hard to hone her poetic talents. She earned a master of arts degree from the program in 1982.

After completing her work at Illinois State, Steingraber turned back to science. She enrolled in the doctoral (Ph.D.) program in biology at the University of Michigan in Ann Arbor. Her studies focused on the possible causes of cancer. She became especially interested in studying environmental causes for the disease, such as cancer-causing substances in ground water. The Ph.D. that she received in 1989 included a specialty in ecology. Her dissertation, a long research paper that is required to earn a doctoral degree, focused on the impact of pesticides and herbicides on the environment.

In addition to her class work, Steingraber traveled to several foreign lands during the 1980s. She spent long periods of time in such places as East Africa and Central America. In Africa, she spent time with refugees from the civil war in Ethiopia. In addition, she studied the various ways that warfare was polluting the Blue Nile River, one of the country's major waterways. Her findings were recounted in *The Spoils of Famine: Ethiopian Famine Policy and Peasant Agriculture* (1988), a book she wrote with two other authors.

Steingraber's studies and travels made her more aware of political issues. She began to define herself as an activist—a person who works for changes in laws and speaks out against aspects of society that strike them as unfair or immoral. During her years at the University of Michigan, she participated in several protest demonstrations. On one occasion, she served a 10-day jail term for her role in protesting military research on campus. "I was the only activist jailed," she said. "I was given the opportunity to work off my conviction (for disturbing the peace) by washing and waxing police cars, but I refused to compromise."

CAREER HIGHLIGHTS

After graduating, Steingraber took a job as a professor of biology at Columbia College in Chicago. At the same time, she looked for ways to apply her scientific knowledge to the political and environmental issues she found important. "I decided after grad school that I would become a scientist within the activist community," she remembered. She felt that her background in biology "could answer some of the questions that women activists were asking" about potential links between pollution and cancer and other health problems.

In 1993 Steingraber was awarded a prestigious Bunting Fellowship at the Radcliffe Institute for Advanced Studies at Harvard University in Cambridge, Massachusetts. A fellowship is a grant of money that helps pay the recipient's living expenses so they can focus more fully on a certain area of study. As part of her work, she became involved with the Women's Community Cancer Project in nearby Boston. Her work with this organization brought her into contact with other activists and helped her gain more information about the plight of cancer victims all around the country. In 1994 she was appointed a visiting scholar at Boston's Northeastern University.

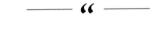

Steingraber found her work to be challenging and rewarding, but it never caused her to abandon her poetry. In fact, she devoted a good deal of her free time to creating new poetic works. Many of these poems were gathered together in *Post-Diagnosis*, a collection of verse that was published in 1995. The book provides readers with a poetic view of a cancer victim's experiences. Some poems concentrate on the details of medical procedures such as bone scans. Others take a

"I was looking for a close examination of all the lines of evidence linking cancer and the environment. When I realized that there was no such book out there, I decided to write it myself."

larger view of the subject, working in references to nuclear testing and atomic accidents. In *Women's Review of Books*, reviewer Adrian Oktenberg expressed some reservations: "The book retains the feeling of an intellectual construction—not necessarily the most desirable feeling for a book of poetry." But Oktenberg also noted that "its subject-matter is so sensitively handled and of such importance that it should still have a wide audience."

Steingraber enjoyed writing poetry, but her next writing project was of an entirely different sort. She began a new book, called *Living Downstream*, after realizing that she could not find an existing book with answers to the questions she had about cancer. "I was looking for a close examination of all the lines of evidence linking cancer and the environment," she recalled. "When I realized that there was no such book out there, I decided to write it myself."

Steingraber's book Living Downstream *reflected her interest in exploring the links between environmental pollution and human health.*

Cancer and Its Causes

To understand the ideas Steingraber explores in *Living Downstream*, it is helpful to understand some of the general characteristics of cancer, as well as its causes. Cancer occurs when cells begin to divide in an abnormal manner, forming tumors. If the growth cannot be stopped, the tumor will impair the functioning of the part of the body where it is found. Malignant (harmful) cell growth can also spread from one area of the body to another. When cancer prevents vital organs from doing their job, the victim dies.

A basic question in cancer research is what causes the cells to begin to grow in a harmful manner. In some cases, cancer is thought to be caused by genetics—the genes that people inherit from their parents make them more likely to develop cancer. In other cases, the person's lifestyle is a contributing factor. For example, scientists have established direct links between smoking and cancer.

"I'm convinced that the increase [in cancer rates] is due to environmental contamination," Steingraber stated. *"We're in the middle of a cancer epidemic."*

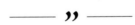

A third potential cause of cancer is environment: the air we breathe, the water we drink and bathe in, and the water and soil that nourish the foods that we eat. This last area of research was the one that most interested Steingraber, for it grew out of her own experience. Doctors had always claimed that genetic factors were the primary reason why so many members of her family had been stricken with cancer. But since Steingraber was adopted, she shared no genes with her adoptive mother or her aunts and uncles who had been diagnosed with cancer. This led her to believe that environmental factors might be the root cause not only of her own struggles with cancer, but also of her family's battles with the disease.

Living Downstream

Living Downstream, first published in 1997, begins with a description of the geography of central Illinois. Steingraber then details the various forms of chemical contamination that have taken place in the region, including contamination from substances that are known carcinogens (things that cause cancer). Though Steingraber focuses on Illinois, she notes that similar hazards are found throughout the United States.

The book's main argument is that pollution of various sorts is responsible for the dramatic rise in the number of cancer cases in the United States in the past 50 years. According to Steingraber's research, in the 1950s approximately 25 percent of Americans could expect to be diagnosed with cancer in their lifetimes. By century's end, however, Steingraber reported that "about 40 percent of us (38.3 percent of women and 48.2 percent of men) will contract the disease sometime within our lifespans." Steingraber notes that this rise in cancer rates occurred at the same time that chemicals became widely used in agriculture and industry. "I'm convinced that the increase is due to environmental contamination," she declared. "We're in the middle of a cancer epidemic."

The idea that certain chemicals can be harmful is not new. As Steingraber points out in her book, the World Health Organization has stated that "at least 80 percent of all cancer is attributable to environmental influences." But *Living Downstream* was important because it collected the environmental data together in one place and brought these facts to the attention of a wide audience. Steingraber's other purpose in writing the book was to urge the American people to take action. She claims that people should pressure government agencies to take much stronger steps to remove known carcinogens from the environment and to test other chemicals to find out if they may cause cancer. "We know cancer is caused by carcinogens," she said. "Therefore we remove carcinogens from our environment, and we prevent cancer. That's the right thing to do."

Throughout the book, Steingraber refers to the famous ecologist and biologist Rachel Carson, author of the 1962 book *Silent Spring.* Carson was a pioneer in drawing attention to dangerous chemicals and their impact on the environment. Indeed, the facts presented in *Silent Spring* resulted in a nationwide ban in the use of the insecticide DDT, which was endangering many bird species. Steingraber finds hope in Carson's experience, but she also discusses Carson's death from breast cancer in 1964, only two years after the publication of her famous book. (For more information on Carson, see *Biography Today Environmental Leaders, Vol. 1.*)

Finding Poetry in Science

In making its arguments, *Living Downstream* presents a lot of scientific information and a lot of statistics. It could have been a very dry book, but Steingraber called on some of the tools she had learned as a poet to make her subject understandable and interesting for non-experts. In a review in the *Chicago Tribune*, Colin Crawford praised "Steingraber's ability to describe complicated scientific information clearly" and her gift for using interesting language and imagery. *Dollars & Sense* reviewer Peter Montague, meanwhile, found that Steingraber is "among the rarest of scientists—those who see the extraordinary among the ordinary and who can write so well that her readers are transported effortlessly through the complexities of an arcane topic like cell biology."

The subject of what can and should be done about environmental hazards is controversial. Few scientific studies have shown a definite link between environmental factors and cancer. The lack of conclusive proof has led some scientists and politicians to say that no changes are necessary until further study is completed. Steingraber strongly disagrees. She notes that obtaining absolute proof of the link between pollution and cancer is virtually impossible, because doing so would require researchers to purposely expose humans to life-threatening chemicals. Moreover, she notes that American communities and neighborhoods with high cancer rates are frequently located in areas with serious pollution problems. *Living Downstream* argues that action needs to be taken immediately to safeguard humans from environmental contamination.

> **"**
>
> *"I am an ecologist. I spend a lot of time thinking about how living things interact with the environments they inhabit. When I became pregnant at age 38, I realized, with amazement, that I myself had become a habitat."*
>
> **"**

Living Downstream brought Steingraber several prestigious awards. *Ms.* magazine named her Woman of the Year in 1997. That same year, President Bill Clinton appointed her to the board for the National Action Plan on Breast Cancer. One year later she was honored with the Will Solimene Award from the New England Chapter of the American Medical Association, the Altman Award from the Jennifer Altman Foundation, and the Medical Communications Award from the American Medical Writers Association. She also was awarded a temporary Writer in Residence position at Illinois Weleyan University, where she had received her undergraduate degree 17 years before.

Having Children and *Having Faith*

In September 1998 Steingraber and her husband, Jeffrey de Castro, welcomed their first child into the world. The arrival of her daughter, Faith Kathryn de Castro, provided Steingraber with a new perspective on the environmental issues that she had been studying. This analysis became

Steingraber enjoys a light moment with her daughter, Faith.

the subject of her next book, *Having Faith: An Ecologist's Journey to Motherhood* (2001). "I am an ecologist," she writes in the preface. "I spend a lot of time thinking about how living things interact with the environments they inhabit. When I became pregnant at age 38, I realized, with amazement, that I myself had become a habitat."

Building on this recognition, Steingraber uses *Having Faith* to investigate the impact that environmental contaminants can have on babies, both before and after birth. "Whatever is in the world's water is in the womb's water," she explained in an online essay entitled "Protecting the First Environment." "Whatever exists in the outside environment—in the potato fields and dairy farms, in chicken eggs and drinking water wells—existed also in the interior environment of my uterus, with its precious population of one." In other words, pollution in the air and water is absorbed by the mother and transferred to the child through the amniotic fluid and the placenta. When the elements that are transferred from mother to fetus are harmful, they can have a harmful effect on the baby's development. Steingraber has noted that many people imagine that the womb "provides absolute protection to the fetus. . . . But in fact the placenta is an open doorway. While it's a very good barrier for keeping out infectious diseases, it doesn't serve that purpose when it comes to toxic chemicals."

Investigating Tainted Milk

The book also explains that the danger of chemical contamination continues after the child is born, because the mother may inadvertently pass harmful substances to the baby through breastfeeding. In these cases, mothers who ingest toxins in air, water, and food pass these chemicals on to their infants through their breast milk. "When it comes to persistent organic pollutants (POPs), breast milk is the most contaminated of all human foods," Steingraber writes. "Indeed, prevailing levels of chemical contaminants in human milk often exceed legally allowable limits in commercial foodstuffs."

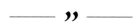

"The question is not whether we should feed our babies chemically contaminated, yet clearly superior, breast milk or chemically uncontaminated, yet clearly inferior, formula. The question is, what do we need to do to get chemical contaminants out of clearly superior breast milk?"

Despite these dangers, Steingraber stresses the advantages of feeding an infant breast milk rather than formula. One of the most important functions of breast milk is that it provides the baby immunity to diseases and helps it develop its permanent immune system. *Having Faith* details Steingraber's decision to breastfeed her child after concluding that the benefits outweighed the risks. "The question is not whether we should feed our babies chemically contaminated, yet clearly superior, breast milk or chemically uncontaminated, yet clearly inferior, formula. The question is, what do we need to do to get chemical contaminants out of clearly superior breast milk?" Steingraber thus returns to one of *Living Downstream*'s dominant themes: that political action is necessary to remove carcinogens from the environment.

Though *Having Faith* contains a serious message and a large amount of scientific information, much of the book recounts Steingraber's personal journey as a mother, with plenty of touching and amusing anecdotes included. This combination, along with Steingraber's literary skills, earned the book positive reviews. *Science* reviewer George M. Woodwell called Steingraber "a brilliantly skilled artisan of image and language" who has "lucid command of much larger realms of science, scholarship, and human nature than most of us manage." *Whole Earth* magazine, meanwhile, praised the book for "brilliantly integrating a touchingly personal story with the data about the polluted ecosystem faced by mothers and children the world over." And *Publishers Weekly* declared that "Steingraber offers the commonest of stories — how she got pregnant, gave birth, and fed her baby — in a most uncommon way. . . . Parents to be or anyone concerned with environmental pollution will want to read and discuss this — and act."

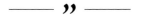

> **Publishers Weekly** *declared that in* **Having Faith** *"Steingraber offers the commonest of stories — how she got pregnant, gave birth, and fed her baby — in a most uncommon way. . . . Parents to be or anyone concerned with environmental pollution will want to read and discuss this — and act."*

A New Home

In 1999 Steingraber and her family moved from Boston to Ithaca, New York, where she became Visiting Assistant Professor at Cornell University. She accepted a position in the Breast Cancer and Environmental Risk Factors Program at the university's Center for the Environment. In 2003 she began working at nearby Ithaca College, where she was named Distinguished Visiting Scholar in the Division of Interdisciplinary and International Studies. The move to Ithaca allowed the family to trade a city apartment for a log cabin in the country. Steingraber was delighted with the move. "I can decipher most countrysides," she writes in *Having Faith*. "I can read something into the architecture of the trees and the direction of the prevailing wind. My intuition works better in the rural world."

Steingraber's new job responsibilities and growing family (a second child was born in 2001) kept her very busy. But her interest in environmental activism and education remained strong. She continued to promote environmental awareness in public speeches around the world, and in 2002

HAVING *Faith*

AN ECOLOGIST'S
JOURNEY TO MOTHERHOOD

"A fascinating journey into how women
move through the often toxic terrain of
pregnancy to the world of child
nourishment and protection."
—*Newsday*

SANDRA STEINGRABER author of *Living Downstream*

In Having Faith, *Steingraber discusses the challenges of maintaining a healthy
pregnancy in a world filled with toxic chemicals.*

109

she appeared on the PBS television program "Now with Bill Moyers" to discuss the effects of chemicals on child development. She used this appearance to emphasize the importance of limiting fetal exposure to toxic chemicals, especially during periods of rapid fetal brain growth. "You can actually paralyze migrating brain cells and extinguish human intelligence," she stated. "Here's where the science is really just beginning to emerge. Maybe certain problems that we understand in the school systems as attention deficit disorders, hyperactivity, the inability to pay attention, aggressive and violent behaviors might have their origins during those windows of vulnerability during pregnancy. And these are questions just being asked. Data are just beginning to come in."

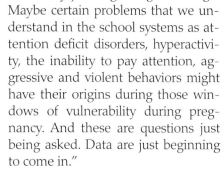

"Children have home and garden pesticides in their urine and they're peeing out wood preservatives," noted Steingraber. *"Women have termite poisons and toilet deodorizers and flame-retardents in their breast milk. . . . We can't continue in the direction we are going. It is essentially premeditated murder."*

Steingraber is considering several different subjects for her next book, including a detailed examination of childhood exposure to toxic substances. Whatever topic she next addresses, it is certain that she will continue to push for changes in the way chemicals and other toxic substances are manufactured and regulated. She admits that accomplishing these changes may require a significant change in the way people relate to the natural world. "The task now is to create an earth-honoring culture founded on the sanctity of life and the sacred human-nature relationship," she stated. "By restoring the earth, we restore ourselves."

Steingraber also believes that if these changes are not made, deaths from cancer will remain much higher than they would in a pollution-free environment. "[Today's] children have home and garden pesticides in their urine and they're peeing out wood preservatives," she said. "Women have termite poisons and toilet deodorizers and flame-retardents in their breast milk. . . . We can't continue in the direction we are going. It is essentially premeditated murder. We don't know who the victims are, but we know that when you release certain chemicals into the environment, a certain number of people are going to get cancer and die because of that. That is just wrong."

MARRIAGE AND FAMILY

Steingraber married Brian Wayne Burt in 1982. They were divorced in 1994. She married Jeffrey de Castro, a sculptor, in 1996. They have two children, Faith Kathryn (born in 1998) and Elijah Jeffrey (born in 2001). The family lives in Ithaca, New York.

HOBBIES AND OTHER INTERESTS

Steingraber enjoys outdoor activities, including hiking, camping, running, and bird-watching.

WRITINGS

The Spoils of Famine: Ethiopian Famine Policy and Peasant Agriculture, 1988 (with Jason W. Clay and Peter Niggli)
Post-Diagnosis (poetry), 1995
Living Downstream: An Ecologist Looks at Cancer and the Environment, 1997 (reprinted in 1998 as *Living Downstream: A Scientist's Personal Investigation of Cancer and the Environment*)
Having Faith: An Ecologist's Journey to Motherhood, 2001

HONORS AND AWARDS

Woman of the Year (*Ms.* Magazine): 1997
Altman Award (Jennifer Altman Foundation): 1998
Will Solimene Award (New England Chapter of the American Medical Association): 1998
Medical Communications Award (American Medical Writers Association): 1998
Rachel Carson Leadership Award (Chatham College): 2001

FURTHER READING

Books

Becher, Anne. *American Environmental Leaders from Colonial Times to the Present*, Vol. 2, 2000
Steingraber, Sandra. *Living Downstream: An Ecologist Looks at Cancer and the Environment*, 1997
Steingraber, Sandra. *Having Faith: An Ecologist's Journey to Motherhood*, 2001
Who's Who in America, 2003

Periodicals

Chicago Tribune, Apr. 24, 1994, p.3; July 20, 1997, p.7; Dec. 23, 2001, p.5;
   May 5, 2002, p.3
Dollars & Sense, July-Aug. 1998, p.37
Ms., Jan.-Feb. 1998, p.68
Multinational Monitor, Mar. 1998, p.20
Providence (RI) Journal-Bulletin, Dec. 24, 1997, p.A1
Public Health Reports, May-June, 1998, p.281
Publishers Weekly, Sep. 24, 2001, p.78
Science, Feb. 1, 2002, p.803
Syracuse (NY) Post-Standard, Apr. 22, 2000, p.A1
Toronto Star, Jan. 16, 2003, p.K6
USA Today, June 18, 1997, p.D8
Utne Reader May-June, 2001, p.60
Whole Earth, Spring 2002, p.29

Online Articles

http://www.pbs.org/now/transcript/transcript117_full.html
   (*NOW with Bill Moyers,* "Kids and Chemicals: Are We Making Our
   Children Sick?" May 17, 2002)

Online Databases

Biography Resource Center Online, 2003, article from *Contemporary Authors
Online,* 2001

ADDRESS

Sandra Steingraber
Gannett Center
Ithaca College
Ithaca, NY 14850

WORLD WIDE WEB SITE

http://www.steingraber.com

RETROSPECTIVE

Edward Teller 1908-2003

Hungarian-American Physicist
Lead Researcher in the Development of the
Atomic Bomb
Main Architect of the Hydrogen Bomb

BIRTH

Edward Teller was born on January 15, 1908, in Budapest, Hungary, which was then the capital city of the Austro-Hungarian Empire. Edward's father was Max Teller, a lawyer. His mother was Ilona Teller, who spent her days caring for Edward and his older sister Emmi.

YOUTH

Teller spent his early years in a comfortable and close-knit Budapest neighborhood. His parents, who were Jewish, were members of a sizeable middle-class community of Jewish professionals and intellectuals in the city, and they provided their children with a safe and secure home environment.

Teller did not speak his first words until he was about four years old, much later than most young children begin using language. When he finally began speaking, however, his words came out clearly and in full sentences. Teller also displayed an unusually strong interest in mathematics as a youngster. In fact, he sometimes became so preoccupied with figuring out math problems in his head that he asked his family not to speak to him at the dinner table. "It was more of a plea than rudeness," his sister recalled. "We knew he was thinking about something he considered very important at the time, and we understood." As he grew older, Teller's keen interest in schoolwork and intellectual challenges sometimes made him the target of harassment from bullies. After a while, though, he learned to tie a leather strap around his schoolbooks and swing the package in a wide arc to fend off his tormentors.

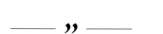

> *As a child, Teller became so preoccupied with figuring out math problems in his head that he asked his family not to speak to him at the dinner table. "It was more of a plea than rudeness," his sister recalled. "We knew he was thinking about something he considered very important at the time, and we understood."*

Teller was very close to his mother, who anxiously watched over her children's safety. Teller recalled that when the family visited the beach, his mother tied ropes around their waists and sat on the shore tightly clutching the other ends of the ropes in her fists. Teller's relationship with his father, on the other hand, was distant and formal. They did enjoy playing chess together from the time Teller was about six. When Edward finally won his first game after years of defeat, however, he blurted out an insult about his father's chess skills. "His reaction shocked me," remembered Teller. "He was hurt. And I was ashamed. I do not believe we ever played chess together again."

With each passing year, young Teller's passion for math and science grew. At age 12, Teller was taken by his father to meet Leopold Klug, a noted professor of mathematics at the University of Budapest. Klug met with

Teller on several other occasions, each time asking him questions that were "far beyond my ability to solve," Teller remembered. "In attempting what was unreachable, I received my first painless lessons in the activity that I liked best. I fell in love with the underlying simplicity of what seems at first complex." Teller's intelligence and passion for math impressed Klug so much that the professor encouraged him to pursue mathematics as a career.

Years of War and Revolution

Teller's love for math and science blossomed at a time when world events cast his family's safety and welfare into doubt. When Teller was born, Hungary was part of the Austro-Hungarian Empire, which had long ruled over southeastern Europe and the Balkan states. In the early years of the 20th century, however, political unrest between a wealthy Hungarian minority and angry ethnic groups—including Slovenes, Croats, Romanians, and Slovaks—kept the area in constant turmoil. In 1914 the simmering conflict boiled over into an all-out war that involved many other nations. In this conflict, which came to be known as World War I, Austria-Hungary and Germany led a coalition of countries against allied forces led by France, England, and the United States. By 1918, when the war ended in victory by the allied forces, Hungary was a poor and battered country.

Hungary continued to struggle during the post-World War I years. In 1919 the nation's government was nearly taken over by communists—people devoted to installing a political system in which the central government controls businesses and many other aspects of society. The communists were defeated, however, by forces led by Admiral Miklós Horthy. Horthy installed a fascist government—a total dictatorship—that remained in place for the next quarter-century. Horthy's government was strongly "anti-Semitic," or hostile toward Jewish people. It placed all sorts of restrictions on the rights of Hungarian Jews, even going so far as to prohibit them from holding certain jobs. Teller's family tried to adjust to these unfair policies, but with each passing year their place in Hungarian society seemed less secure.

EDUCATION

Teller was an excellent student with a tremendous appetite for learning about the world around him. At age 18, he even won first place in a nationwide high school mathematics contest. He spent much of his free time reading as well, which further fueled his interest in math and science.

Teller during his days as a research associate at the University of Göttingen in Germany.

When Teller graduated from high school in 1925, he wanted to continue his schooling so that he could become a professor of mathematics. His father, however, reminded him that a professor's salary was very low. He also worried that the government's employment rules might make it impossible for his son to win a faculty position with a Hungarian university. After many arguments, the Teller men settled on a compromise. Edward enrolled as an engineering student at the University of Budapest in 1925 and continued to live at home. Within a year, however, Teller transferred to the Institute of Technology in Karlsruhe, Germany, to study both engineering and mathematics. "I studied virtually all the time," Teller recalled. At Karlsruhe Teller found a thriving community of scientists and scholars. He soon developed relationships with some of the most important scientists of the day, including J. Robert Oppenheimer, Niels Bohr, Hans Bethe, I. I. Rabi, Eugene Wigner, Leo Szilard, and John A. Wheeler. Years later, many of these men worked with Teller in the United States to develop the world's first atomic bomb.

During Teller's college years, he grew increasingly fascinated with a developing field of study called physics—the study of matter and energy and the ways in which they interact. In 1928 he transferred to the University of Munich, Germany, as a physics student. Not long after his move to Munich, Teller suffered a terrible accident. Leaping from a moving streetcar, he slipped and fell. His foot was crushed and partially severed. As Teller recalled the accident, "I saw my boot lying there, and I wondered, 'How will I go hiking?'" He underwent an innovative operation that removed the front part of his foot and allowed him to walk on the padded stump of his foot.

After a short stay at the University of Munich, Teller moved to the University of Leipzig. He studied under Werner Heisenberg, who would later become known as one of the greatest physicists of the 20th century. Teller became part of a group of bright young students who traveled with Heisenberg to meet prestigious scientists all over Europe. In 1930, at the young age of 22, Teller earned his doctorate in physics.

FIRST JOBS

After earning his doctorate, Teller took a job as a research associate in 1930 at the University of Göttingen in Germany. But Germany had become so strongly anti-Semitic by this time that he doubted that he could ever build a successful career there. With this in mind, he moved to England in 1932 to teach physics at the University of London. In 1934 he won a Rockefeller Foundation fellowship that allowed him to work at the Institute for Theoretical Physics in Copenhagen for eight months. Teller considered his experience in Copenhagen, where he worked alongside noted physicist Niels Bohr, "among the most important and wonderful periods of my life."

In 1935 Teller left Copenhagen and returned to teaching chemistry at the University of London. But a short time later, Teller was offered a professorship in the physics department of George Washington University in Washington, D.C. Teller jumped at the opportunity. With political turmoil and anti-Semitism on the rise in Europe, he saw that it was a good time for scientists — especially Jewish scientists — to move to the United States.

Under the guidance of George Gamow, the school's physics department had emerged as a stimulating and supportive environment for work in theoretical physics. In fact, great physicists from around the globe flocked to the school to pursue their research. Not surprisingly, Teller greatly enjoyed his years at the school. He and his wife, Mici, regularly opened their home to visiting scientists, and Teller developed a reputation as a generous host who loved scholarly companionship. "There were always people in their house," recalled physicist Hans Bethe. "It soon got about in the local community that Teller was interested in the whole gamut of chemical and physical problems, that he was happy to talk about your problems, and that you would come away with some new approach or a new avenue through your specific maze," added scientist Alfred Sklar.

Teller stayed at George Washington University from 1935 to 1941. During this time, he focused much of his research efforts on the behavior of matter in different environments, including the interior of stars. He also worked with Gamow to study radioactivity — the process by which certain

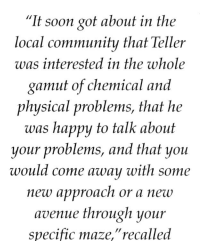

"It soon got about in the local community that Teller was interested in the whole gamut of chemical and physical problems, that he was happy to talk about your problems, and that you would come away with some new approach or a new avenue through your specific maze," recalled scientist Alfred Sklar.

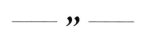

atoms or isotopes (one of two or more atoms with the same number of protons but different numbers of neutrons) spontaneously emit energetic particles when their nuclei disintegrate. Their groundbreaking work became known as the Gamow-Teller selection rules for "beta decay"—the process by which an element's nucleus is transformed from one type of nucleon (proton or neutron) to another.

CAREER HIGHLIGHTS

By the time Teller immigrated to the United States in 1935, he was already regarded as a brilliant young physicist. As a respected professor and the author or co-author of nearly 30 research papers, he achieved more by his 30th birthday than many researchers do in their entire lifetimes. But these accomplishments merely set the stage for Teller to play a major role in three events that proved central to world history in the 20th century: the development of the atomic bomb in 1945; the creation of the hydrogen bomb in the 1950s; and the debate over the United States' Strategic Defense Initiative (SDI) missile defense system in the 1980s, the so-called "Star Wars" system.

The Dawn of the Atomic Age

As Teller established his reputation as a bright physicist in the United States, scientists back in Europe made a startling discovery that forever changed the course of Teller's life. In 1938 German chemists Otto Hahn and Fritz Strassmann became the first scientists to split the atom. This accomplishment attracted the notice of scientists around the world. They recognized that nuclear fission—as the splitting of an atom came to be called—released enormous amounts of energy. If controlled, this process could be used to create weapons with almost unimaginable destructive power. The prospect that Germany might be the first to create such "atomic" weapons alarmed many scientists and lawmakers. Led by Adolf Hitler, the Nazi Party had transformed Germany into a threatening military power and a center of vicious anti-Semitism by the late 1930s.

A portrait of University of Chicago scientists who helped develop the atomic bomb, including Teller (back row, far left) and Enrico Fermi (front row, second from right).

Teller used his growing influence to help persuade the U.S. government to support atomic research and the development of new weaponry. In August 1939, Teller and two other scientists convinced famous scientist Albert Einstein to compose a letter to U.S. President Franklin D. Roosevelt in support of such research. This famous letter warned that "the element uranium may be turned into a new and important source of energy in the immediate future. . . . This new phenomenon would also lead to the construction of . . . extremely powerful bombs of a new type."

It took nearly ten weeks before the letter reached the president. By this time the threat of Nazi power had become very clear: Germany had invaded neighboring Poland on September 1, 1939. A short time later, Hitler and Soviet leader Joseph Stalin had divided Poland between themselves. By the end of the year, Germany was at war with England, France, and other nations. This conflict, which came to be known as World War II, eventually widened to include nations all over the world.

In the weeks following the German invasion of Poland, President Roosevelt set up an Advisory Committee on Uranium. Teller was among the scientists assembled to discuss how to proceed. As a result of this initial meeting, the government approved its first funding for research on nuclear fission, at Columbia University in New York. It was the first step in an atomic energy development program that eventually cost the United States $2 billion.

The Manhattan Project

Teller was intrigued by the idea of atomic energy and despised the threat of Nazi domination, but he was not sure he wanted to leave his teaching job for a bomb-making project. On May 10, 1940, however, President Roosevelt told the Eighth Pan American Scientific Congress in Washington that "without the work of the scientists, the war and the world would be lost." Though he sat in a huge crowd of people, Teller felt as though the president was speaking directly to him. He immediately made up his mind to help the war effort. Using his skills as a scientist to provide security for his adopted nation remained his professional focus from that time forward.

Roosevelt soon expanded the Uranium Committee into the National Defense Research Committee. Their research on what would become the atomic bomb was supervised by what was officially called the Manhattan Engineer District, but commonly referred to as the "Manhattan Project." The work of the Manhattan Project was carried out in laboratories at Columbia University, the University of Chicago, Princeton University in New Jersey, and the University of California at Berkley. On December 7, 1941, Japan — which had allied itself with Germany in World War II — launched a surprise bombing attack on the U.S. naval base at Pearl Harbor, Hawaii. This event drew the United States into World War II and convinced the U.S. government to centralize the main work of the Manhattan Project in a secret laboratory underneath the football stadium at the University of Chicago. Remembering the bombing of Pearl Harbor, Teller said that "Overnight, every trace of opposition to the war had disappeared. Everyone's commitment was now whole-hearted, open, and complete."

From this point forward, the members of the Manhattan Project worked feverishly to develop a bomb that could shift the tide of the war in favor of the United States and its allies. The research on nuclear fission was top secret. No one wanted to take the chance that secrets could reach the Germans and give them an edge in building the world's first atomic weapons. As a result, Teller and others working on the project were subjected to intense security precautions.

When research was centralized in Chicago, many of the scientists Teller had been working with in New York were asked to relocate. But Teller initially was told to stay in New York. U.S. security officials recognized that Teller and his wife had become U.S. citizens in 1941. But the Manhattan Project's supervisors were concerned that they might be a security risk, since their families remained in enemy territory. Teller was denied access to the project until the late spring of 1942, when J. Robert Oppenheimer took responsibility for the theoretical study of weapon design at the Manhattan Project. He quickly obtained the necessary security clearance for Teller and several other scientists to join the project in Chicago. Teller soon developed a close working relationship with the brilliant Italian-born physicist Enrico Fermi.

"The road up the mesa [at Los Alamos] was barely passable; once we were on top we were confined to the immediate grounds by barbed wire," recalled Teller. "Our badges were checked by guards when we entered; our mail was censored; our privacy became a distant memory."

In 1943, the Manhattan Project, now called "Project Y," moved to new facilities in the largely uninhabited southwestern desert near Los Alamos, New Mexico. The army constructed the laboratory at the site of a small, private preparatory school. Only 30 people moved to the site at first, but by 1945 nearly 10,000 people populated Los Alamos. Teller was among the first scientists to make the move. At Los Alamos the lives and the work of the scientists were closely watched. "The road up the mesa was barely passable; once we were on top we were confined to the immediate grounds by barbed wire," Teller remembered. "Our badges were checked by guards when we entered; our mail was censored; our privacy became a distant memory."

Dropping the Bomb

Working at a frantic pace, the scientists at Los Alamos created an experimental atomic bomb called Trinity. On the night of July 16, 1945, scientists assembled about 20 miles away from the blast site near Alamogordo, New Mexico. To protect himself from the radiation and the brilliant light he ex-

Teller speaks at a physics meeting of the American Association for the Advancement of Science in 1954.

pected from the bomb's blast, Teller coated himself in sun lotion and donned welder's glasses and heavy gloves. When the bomb was detonated, the explosion created an enormous glowing blue mushroom cloud and such intense heat that the scientists felt it from their distant location. The scientists then left the test site "with hardly a word," Teller recalled. "We knew that the next nuclear explosion would not be an experiment." Indeed, the United States dropped the first atomic bomb on the Japanese city of Hiroshima on August 6, 1945. Three days later, it dropped another atomic bomb on the Japanese city of Nagasaki. In total, about 250,000 people were killed by the two bombs. The Japanese soon surrendered. Their surrender, combined with the defeat of Germany's armed forces a few months earlier, finally brought World War II to a close.

The United States had won the race to create an atomic bomb, but the world was shocked and disturbed by its awesome power. Debates raged over the morality of using weapons capable of such mass destruction of life. People also worried about the safety of a world in which opposing armies could use such weapons on civilian populations. The debate over the use of atomic weapons intensified even more after Russia developed its own atomic weapons. The United States and the Soviet Union, locked after 1947 into a struggle for world supremacy known as the Cold War, each developed huge arsenals of atomic weapons. It was the Cold War that kept Teller involved in weapons research for the rest of his career.

Back in Los Alamos, the future of the weapons laboratory was uncertain. Would it be a centralized lab for new energy research, or simply a place to produce more atomic bombs? While government officials pondered the question, Teller returned to Chicago in 1946. Late that same year, President Harry S. Truman appointed an Atomic Energy Commission (AEC) to develop further military and peacetime applications for atomic energy.

During this period, many scientists came to believe that nuclear fission could be harnessed to produce low-cost energy for American industry and households. In 1947 Teller joined an AEC subcommittee responsible for assessing the safety of nuclear reactors — large power plants that would run on nuclear energy. He served as chairman of the subcommittee, called the Reactor Safeguard Committee (RSC) for the next six years. In 1953 the RSC merged with another committee to form the Advisory Committee on Reactor Safeguards. Teller stayed on as a member of this committee until 1955. In the meantime, he also became heavily involved in research work on an even more powerful type of weapon — the hydrogen bomb.

Developing the Hydrogen Bomb

Not long after scientists began work on the atomic bomb, Teller and some others began to research the possibility of mastering the process of nuclear fusion. This process is the opposite of fission; it involves fusing together the nuclei of isotopes of atoms such as hydrogen. Theoretically, this process could release even more energy than fission, and at a fraction of the cost. Scientists had extensive experience working with deuterium, also known as heavy hydrogen, because it contained nuclei that fused very easily. "It had become clear that these atomic bombs would be powerful but expensive," explained Teller. "If deuterium could be ignited, it would give a much less expensive fuel." But not all scientists were excited about this new research direction. Some worried that the explosion of a hydrogen bomb might ignite heavy hydrogen and other elements in the earth's atmosphere, perhaps incinerating the entire world.

Questions about the possibilities and dangers of nuclear fusion remained in the background during the early and mid-1940s, when government scientists were focused on building an atomic bomb. But after the successful completion of the atomic bomb, the scientists turned their attention to the issue of nuclear fusion. Teller became a steadfast supporter of further investigation, but others were vehemently opposed to further study. In November 1949, the General Advisory Committee of the AEC issued a critical report that emphasized the risks of such research. Teller was angered by the report, which in his words concluded that "as long as you people work very hard and diligently to make a better atomic bomb, you are doing a fine job; but if you succeed in making real progress toward another kind of nuclear explosion, you are doing something immoral."

> "One of my main reasons for working on the hydrogen bomb was its novelty. Not knowing how it would influence the future, I wanted both as a scientist and also for practical reasons to know how it would work."

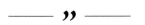

In 1949 Teller predicted that if the U.S. government actively supported research efforts in Los Alamos, a hydrogen bomb, or "H-bomb," could be ready for testing by 1951. In 1950 President Truman announced the government's full support of continued work on "all forms of atomic weapons, including the so-called hydrogen or superbomb." Teller was subsequently appointed chairman of the Los Alamos thermonuclear program, which meant that he supervised research efforts on the H-bomb.

The U.S. government's decision to build a hydrogen bomb angered and frightened many people. Some prominent scientists publicly denounced further research on the H-bomb and other atomic weapons. Ordinary citizens demonstrated against this type of weapons research as well, convinced that it would lead to a deadly arms race between the United States and the Soviet Union. But Teller never hesitated in his commitment to his research. He argued that it would be better for the world if the United States developed the H-bomb before the Soviets, who were also trying to develop such a weapon. He also claimed that the quest to build a hydrogen bomb was in essence a quest for knowledge. "One of my main reasons for working on the hydrogen bomb was its novelty," he said. "Not knowing how it would influence the future, I wanted both as a scientist and also for practical reasons to know how it would work." On May 8, 1951, a test blast known as the George Test completely vaporized an iron and concrete structure placed on an isolated Pacific island. The blast proved that nuclear fusion could be accomplished on earth without destroying the planet.

H-Bomb Success at Lawrence Livermore National Laboratory

The successful test blast did not end the controversy swirling around H-bomb construction, however. Scientists and politicians remained deeply divided over the wisdom of moving forward. At an Atomic Energy Commission conference held shortly after the test blast, bomb opponents controlled the program and refused to allow Teller to speak. Frustrated after listening to days of discussion, Teller finally insisted on being heard. In a memorable display of debating brilliance, Teller reportedly convinced many doubtful members of the audience that moving ahead with the development of hydrogen-based weapons was a necessary course of action.

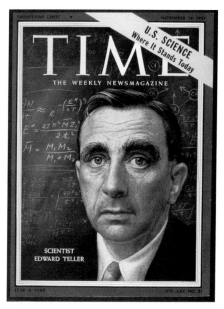

In November 1957, Teller's contributions to American science landed him on the cover of Time.

By this time, however, the research team was deeply divided. Frustrated by this development, Teller resigned from his post at Los Alamos on November 1, 1951, and returned to the University of Chicago. During the winter he spoke with powerful people in the government and the military, including esteemed scientist Ernest Lawrence, about the possibility of building a second government-sponsored research laboratory. Backed by the Air Force, the National Security Council, and the Atomic Energy Commission, Teller and Lawrence joined together to head the newly created Lawrence Livermore National Laboratory in California. At Lawrence Livermore, Teller once again moved forward with hydrogen bomb plans. He also joined the faculty of the University of California at Berkeley as a professor of physics.

Within a year, Teller and his team had developed a 65-ton hydrogen bomb, the most powerful weapon ever developed. With help from scientists in Los Alamos, researchers placed the bomb on the mile-wide island of Elugelab, in a remote part of the Pacific Ocean. On November 1, 1952, the bomb was detonated, setting off a fireball over three miles wide and a mushroom cloud that reached the top of the stratosphere. The Pacific island of Elugelab was vaporized, removed from the face of the earth, by a bomb more powerful than all of the bombs dropped by Allied forces during World War II, including the atomic bombs, combined.

The development of the H-bomb did not end the terrifying arms race between the Americans and the Soviets, though. Within a year the Soviets had built a hydrogen bomb of their own, and the two superpowers continued to develop ever more powerful weapons for the next 30 years.

"If a person leaves his country, leaves his continent, leaves his relatives, leaves his friends, the only people he knows are his professional colleagues," said Teller. "If more than 90 percent of these then come around to consider him an enemy, an outcast, it is bound to have an effect."

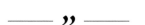

A Controversial Reputation

Teller's hard push to develop the H-bomb, combined with his many public statements concerning the danger posed by the Soviet Union, made him a controversial figure in American life. Debate about his attitudes and actions became even more intense in 1954, when he was called to testify at a hearing regarding his old friend and colleague J. Robert Oppenheimer.

In the early to mid-1950s, work on the hydrogen bomb had proceeded in the United States under a cloud of concern about Communist infiltration of American life. Fears about the "red menace" of Communism were fanned by Senator Joseph McCarthy and others. McCarthy even held Senate hearings into those suspected of Communist beliefs, but little evidence of anti-American Communist activity ever came to light. In 1954 Oppenheimer became ensnared in this tense political environment. A longtime chairman and advisor of the Atomic Energy Commission, Oppenheimer was suspended from his position on charges that his past association with Communists made him a security risk. Today, some historians believe that these charges were politically motivated, primarily because some politicians and military leaders objected to Oppenheimer's support for arms control. They also were unhappy that he seemed to have changed his mind about the wisdom of pursuing H-bomb research.

When Teller was called to testify, he disputed charges that Oppenheimer was disloyal. But he also stated that "I feel that I would like to see the vital interests of this country in hands which I understand better and therefore trust more." Teller's testimony was seen by some members of the scientific

*Teller (right) congratulates J. Robert Oppenheimer (left) after
Oppenheimer received the 1963 Enrico Fermi Award.*

community as a malicious betrayal of his longtime colleague, especially
after Oppenheimer was stripped of his security clearance. As late as 1974,
Teller lamented the impact that the incident had on his relationship with
his peers: "If a person leaves his country, leaves his continent, leaves his
relatives, leaves his friends, the only people he knows are his professional
colleagues. If more than 90 percent of these then come around to consider
him an enemy, an outcast, it is bound to have an effect. . . . The truth is it
had a profound effect." For his part, Oppenheimer eventually cleared his
name, and in 1963 he received the AEC's highest award, the Enrico Fermi
Award.

Teller, meanwhile, continued to work in various capacities at California's
Lawrence Livermore Laboratory. He worked on a variety of projects, from
environmental and bio-medical research projects intended for civilian use
to work on X-ray lasers and particle beams for military purposes. He

Teller (left) was a strong supporter of the Strategic Defense Initiative (SDI), also known as "Star Wars," the defense program that President Ronald Reagan (middle) launched in the 1980s.

served as associate director of the lab from 1960 to 1975, at which time he also ended his teaching career at Berkeley. He continued to serve as a consultant to the lab from 1975 until his death in 2003. During these decades of research, he received many prestigious awards from scientific organizations around the world, including the Enrico Fermi Award (in 1962), the

Groves Gold Medal (1974), the Harvey Prize (1975), the American College of Nuclear Medicine's Gold Medal (1980), the National Medal of Science (1983), and the Sylvanus Thayer Medal of Science (1986).

Star Wars and Beyond

Teller's work at Lawrence Livermore drew him into a number of other military program controversies in his later career. Over time, the massive buildup of atomic and hydrogen (also known as thermonuclear) weapons in the United States and the Soviet Union had led to the development of the policy of mutually assured destruction, or MAD. The MAD policy acknowledged that the two nations had the capacity to completely destroy each other. This compelled them to work through their problems peacefully in order to avoid world destruction.

For years, Teller had been interested in developing defensive weapons systems that might shoot down nuclear warheads launched by the Soviets or other enemies. By the early 1980s, he became a leading supporter of the creation of a Strategic Defense Initiative (SDI). Under this plan, which was nicknamed Star Wars, the United States would launch a program to build and disperse a sophisticated satellite system in outer space. These satellites would be programmed to detect and destroy missiles or other weapons launched at the United States before they could detonate.

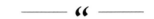

"Through the decades, I have worked for one simple, straightforward purpose, with one simple conviction. This conviction is that in a difficult situation, ignorance will not help. What we need is knowledge — knowledge that atomic explosives could be built (they can), that hydrogen bombs could be built (they can), that defense will now become important (it will)."

Teller believed that developing SDI technology was a sensible response to a quickly changing world. "Through the decades, I have worked for one simple, straightforward purpose, with one simple conviction," he said. "This conviction is that in a difficult situation, ignorance will not help. What we need is knowledge — knowledge that atomic explosives could be built (they can), that hydrogen bombs could be built (they can), that defense will now become important (it will)." Simply attacking a foe, he concluded, was no longer "the one reliable winning move."

Teller won many prestigious awards throughout his career, including the Presidential Medal of Freedom from the U.S. and the Corvin Award, pictured here, from his native Hungary.

The SDI concept was embraced by President Ronald Reagan, who saw the Soviet Union as a serious threat. He soon adopted SDI as a top priority of his presidency. There was great opposition to SDI, however, both in the United States and throughout the world. Some critics argued against the great expense of building such a system. Other detractors pointed to the technical challenges to creating such a system. In addition, some people felt that pursuing SDI would only escalate the arms race — and might even lead the Soviets to launch a nuclear attack before the United States could develop a defensive system. Finally, some critics feared that if such a system could be made operational, it might be used for offensive strikes as well as defensive protection.

In the end, the debate about SDI subsided with the economic collapse of the Soviet Union in 1989. Both superpowers had devoted billions of dollars to weapons research and creation over the years. While the capitalist United States could bear the expense, the costs eventually destroyed the economy of the communist Soviet Union. By the early 1990s the Soviet Union had broken into a variety of smaller states and a still powerful Russia. Though the Russians maintained control of weapons, the tensions that had pitted the two nations against each other in a long Cold War had ended. In 1993 the administration of President Bill Clinton formally announced the end of all funding for the SDI program.

Teller worked diligently until the end of his life as a consultant and advisor at the Lawrence Livermore Lab. He also maintained relations with the University of California at Berkeley, where he had been a professor emeritus since 1975. Just a few months before his death on September 9, 2003, he was awarded the Presidential Medal of Freedom, the nation's highest civilian honor. Teller was deeply touched to receive this honor. "In my long life, I had to face some difficult decisions and found myself often in doubt whether I acted the right way," he said. "Thus the medal is a great blessing for me."

MARRIAGE AND FAMILY

Edward Teller married Augusta Maria "Mici" Harkányi on February 26, 1934, after a nine-year courtship. The uncertainties of World War II worried Mici, who delayed having children until she felt comfortable that the world would be a safe place to raise a family. As soon as the United States entered World War II after the bombing of Pearl Harbor, Mici became certain that Hitler would be defeated. "A few months later, she was pregnant and buying furniture," Teller recalled.

Their son, Paul, was born in February 1943 and grew up to become a philosophy of science professor at the University of Chicago. Their daughter, Wendy, was born in 1946. She studied mathematics at Radcliffe University and took a job with Tellabs, Inc., a large manufacturer of electronic equipment.

Teller's father, mother, and sister survived the Holocaust that killed so many European Jews during World War II, but many other members of his extended family were murdered during this dark period in world history. After World War II they continued to live in Hungary, which fell under the control of the Soviet Union. Teller's father died in 1950. One year later, authorities forcibly relocated his mother and sister from Budapest to a rural hut with no indoor plumbing. They were forced to live there for the next 18 months. Upon their return to Budapest in 1952, Emmi resumed her work as a tutor, but she continued to be harassed by authorities. At one point she was imprisoned for three days and repeatedly questioned about her brother's life and work. Emmi's son, meanwhile, escaped from Hungary in October 1956, and he met his Uncle Edward for the first time in 1957.

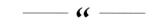

Just a few months before his death on September 9, 2003, Teller was awarded the Presidential Medal of Freedom, the nation's highest civilian honor. He was deeply touched to receive this honor. "In my long life, I had to to face some difficult decisions and found myself often in doubt whether I acted the right way," he said. "Thus the medal is a great blessing for me."

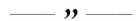

During the 1950s, Teller repeatedly tried to get Hungarian authorities to grant his mother and sister permission to move to the United States. "I tried all kinds of things, but nothing worked," he recalled. About three weeks after mentioning his difficulties to his friend physicist Leo Szilard, however, they were finally granted passports to leave Hungary. They were reunited with Edward Teller in the United States in 1959. Hungarian officials gave no reason for their change of heart, but Teller believed that Szilard used political connections to help his mother and sister leave the country.

HOBBIES AND OTHER INTERESTS

Teller learned to play the piano as a young boy. He was so talented that his mother had fleeting hopes that he might be a concert pianist. But Teller was more interested in math, and he played the piano solely for relaxation. Teller also loved hiking, but the loss of his foot in his early adulthood made scrambling over rocky terrain difficult. He subsequently became a skilled Ping-Pong player.

SELECTED WRITINGS

Raman Effect and Its Chemical Applications, 1939 (with J. H. Hibben)
The Structure of Matter, 1949 (with F. O. Rice)
Our Nuclear Future: Facts, Dangers, and Opportunities, 1958 (with A. L. Latter)
Basic Concepts of Physics, Part 1, 1960
The Legacy of Hiroshima, 1962 (with Allen Brown)
The Reluctant Revolutionary, 1964
Power and Security, 1976
Energy from Heaven and Earth, 1979
Fusion: Magnetic Confinement, 1981
Better a Shield than a Sword: Perspectives on Defense and Technology, 1987
Conversations on the Dark Secrets of Physics, 1991 (with Wendy Teller and Wilson Taley)
Memoirs: A Twentieth-Century Journey in Science and Politics, 2001 (with Judith Shoolery)

HONORS AND AWARDS

Albert Einstein Award: 1959
General Donovan Memorial Award: 1959
Living History Award (Research Institute of America): 1960
Golden Plate Award for American Academic Achievement: 1961
Thomas E. White Award: 1962
Enrico Fermi Award: 1962
Robins Award of America: 1963
Leslie R. Groves Gold Medal: 1974

Harvey Prize: 1975
Semmelweiss Medal: 1977
Albert Einstein Award (Technion Institute of Israel): 1977
ARCS Man of the Year: 1980
Gold Medal (American College of Nuclear Medicine): 1980
Man of the Year (Achievement Rewards for College Scientists): 1980
A.C. Eringen Award (Society of Engineering Science): 1980
Distinguished Scientist Award (National Science Development Board): 1981
National Medal of Science: 1983
Joseph Handleman Prize: 1983
Sylvanus Thayer Medal of Science: 1986
Shelby Cullom Davis Award (Ethics and Public Policy Association): 1988
Presidential Citizen Award: 1989
Ettore Majorana Erice Scienza Per La Pace Award: 1990
Order of Banner with Rubies (Republic of Hungary): 1990
Corvin Award: 2001
Presidential Medal of Freedom: 2003

FURTHER READING

Books

Bankston, John. *Edward Teller and the Development of the Hydrogen Bomb,* 2002 (juvenile)
Blumberg, Stanley A., and Gwinn Ownes. *Energy and Conflict: The Life and Times of Edward Teller,* 1976
Blumberg, Stanley A., and Louis G. Panos. *Edward Teller: Giant of the Golden Age of Physics,* 1990
Kevles, Daniel J. *The Physicists: The History of a Scientific Community in Modern America,* 1978
Notable Twentieth-Century Scientists, 1994
O'Neill, Daniel T. *The Firecracker Boys,* 1994
World of Invention, 1994

Periodicals

Bulletin of the Atomic Scientists, Jan./Feb. 1990, p.23
Life, Sep. 6, 1954, p.61
Nation, Sep. 28, 1992, p.316; Sep. 19, 1994
New Scientist, Sep. 2, 1982; Sep. 21, 1991, p.50
New Statesman & Society, Sep. 30, 1994
Newsweek, Aug. 2, 1954; Oct. 18, 1954

Physics Today, Jan. 1991, p.18; Jan. 1992, p.74; Nov. 2001, p.55
Science, Feb. 1955; Nov. 19, 1982
Scientific American, May 1990
U.S. News and World Report, Feb. 29, 1988, p.1; Nov. 28, 1988, p.8; Aug. 17, 1998, p.64
Washington Post, Jan. 19, 1980; Nov. 18, 1988; Sep. 10, 2003, p.A8; Sep. 11, 2003, p.B6

Online Articles

http://www.achievement.org
(*Academy of Achievement,* "Edward Teller, Ph.D.: Father of the Hydrogen Bomb," Sep. 10, 2003)
http://www.llnl.gov
(*Lawrence Livermore National Laboratory,* "Edward Teller," Nov. 3, 2003)

Online Databases

Biography Resource Center Online, 2003, articles from *American Decades,* 1998; *The Cold War, 1945-1991,* 1992; *Notable Scientists, From 1900 to the Present,* 2001; and *World of Invention,* 1999

Peggy Whitson 1960-

American Astronaut
First Science Officer on the International Space
Station

BIRTH

Peggy Annette Whitson was born on February 9, 1960, in Mt.
Ayr, Iowa. She is the daughter of Earl Keith Whitson and Beth
Avalee (Walters) Whitson, who raised pigs on their 800-acre
Iowa farmstead. She has one brother and one sister.

YOUTH AND EDUCATION

Whitson was raised on her parents' farm outside the small town of Beaconsfield, Iowa. She enjoyed her rural childhood and claimed that her small-town upbringing was essential to her later success. "I wouldn't trade the experience I had growing up in rural Iowa because it was very influential in who I became," she said. Whitson also credited her parents with giving her a strong sense of self-worth and confidence. "The two hardest-working people I know are my parents," she stated. "They always encouraged me, always told me you can do whatever you set your mind to."

"*The two hardest-working people I know are my parents,*"*Whitson stated.* "*They always encouraged me, always told me you can do whatever you set your mind to.*"

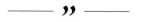

At age nine, Whitson joined the rest of the nation in watching the historic July 1969 Apollo 11 space flight to the moon. She was spellbound by the sight of American astronauts Neil Armstrong and Buzz Aldrin as they left their spacecraft and became the first people to walk on the moon. From that day forward she dreamed of becoming an astronaut herself, even though there were no women in the astronaut corps at that time.

As Whitson grew older, she was a hard-working and dedicated student who competed in basketball and track. She finished second in her class at Mt. Ayr Community High School. During her senior year, she learned that the National Aeronautics and Space Administration (NASA) had finally decided to include women in its astronaut training program. Whitson greeted the news as a sign that her dream of becoming an astronaut might yet become a reality.

After Whitson graduated from high school in 1978, she pursued a course of college study that would help her in her quest to become an astronaut. She knew that most astronauts in the NASA program had piloting or science experience, so she focused on studying biology and chemistry at Iowa Wesleyan College. She took only three years to finish the school's four-year program, graduating summa cum laude ("with high honors") with a bachelor of science degree in 1981. She then enrolled at Rice University in Houston, Texas. She chose to continue her education at Rice primarily because it was located near NASA's Johnson Space Center, a primary facility of the U.S. space program. Whitson studied biochemistry at Rice and received her Ph.D. (doctorate degree) in 1985.

CAREER HIGHLIGHTS

After earning her Ph.D., Whitson worked at Rice University as a postdoctorate fellow. In this position, she could continue to pursue scientific research at the university even though she was no longer working toward a degree. In 1986 she joined NASA's Johnson Space Center as a resident research associate for the National Research Council. That same year, she submitted her first application for admission into NASA's astronaut program. When she was passed over, she did not admit defeat. Instead, she simply prepared another application for the next class. For the next decade, her application was rejected every year. But she never gave up. After each rejection, she filled out another application for the next year's program.

Building a Rewarding Career on Earth

In the meantime, Whitson continued with her research activities at the Johnson Space Center. In 1989 she moved into the job of research biochemist, working directly for NASA. One of her first assignments at NASA was to work with scientists associated with the Russian space program. This gave her the opportunity to make her first visit to Russia in 1989. As the months passed by, Whitson devoted herself to an interesting assortment of studies. For example, she planned and performed experiments that explored how a zero-gravity environment, like the one astronauts experience in space, can affect the body. When space shuttle mission STS-47 flew in September 1992, it carried a special laboratory for experiments. One of those was an experiment on bone cells that Whitson had helped to develop.

In addition to her work with NASA, Whitson became a college instructor. From 1991 to 1997 she served as an adjunct (part-time) assistant professor for the University of Texas medical school, where she taught classes in internal medicine, human biological chemistry, and genetics. In 1997 she became an adjunct assistant professor at Rice University's Mabee Laboratory for Biochemical and Genetic Engineering, a position she continues to hold.

Joining the *Mir* Space Station Project

In 1992 Whitson was named a project scientist for the Space Shuttle-*Mir* project. The *Mir* (Russian for "peace") was a space station operated by the Russian Space Agency that orbited the earth from 1986 to 2001. For much of the life of the *Mir* project, however, NASA contributed funding and scientific expertise to support research aboard the *Mir*. It even used its space

Whitson dreamed of being an astronaut from a very young age.

shuttle program to deliver astronauts and materials to and from the space station.

Whitson's initial responsibility with the *Mir* project was to design scientific experiments that could be performed in the space station's zero-gravity environment. Many of Whitson's experiments focused on determining what astronauts needed to live in space over long periods of time. The missions she supported included the first flight of a Russian cosmonaut on the space shuttle (STS-60, in February 1994); the first approach of the space shuttle to the *Mir* station (STS-63, in February 1995); and the first docking of the space shuttle with *Mir* (STS-71, in June 1995).

In 1993 Whitson was promoted to deputy division chief for NASA's medical sciences division. Two years later she was named co-chair of the U.S./Russian Mission Science Working Group. She took this position at a time when NASA had begun sending American astronauts to live and work on the *Mir* space station for months at a time. Whitson's job was to help supervise and coordinate plans for scientific experiments to be performed on board the *Mir.* She found this work to be both fascinating and rewarding. But she could not help but wish that she might one day be able to conduct the experiments herself, in space.

Joining the Astronaut Corps

In May 1996, ten years of hard work and persistence finally paid off when Whitson was selected for NASA's astronaut corps. Her first task was to complete NASA's two-year training and evaluation program for prospective astronauts. This intense and demanding program included water survival and SCUBA training until she was fully certified as a deep-sea diver. This experience prepared her for NASA's extravehicular activity (EVA) training, which takes place underwater.

As the weeks passed by, Whitson was repeatedly challenged. For example, she was exposed to high- and low-air pressure situations so that doctors could see how her body reacted to these emergency conditions. She also spent time on NASA's "Vomit Comet," a special jet plane that creates conditions of virtual weightlessness (levels close to zero gravity) by making steep, sustained dives. On each flight, Whitson endured as many as 40 separate dives. Finally, she received technical training on the various space shuttle systems, from guidance and navigation to communications. Not only did she learn how to operate these systems, she participated in numerous drills so she could be prepared for any emergency.

> *Whitson was thrilled to learn that she had been assigned to the International Space Station. "I don't think I would have turned down anything, but my first choice was to fly on station. I want to get up there, start doing science, and help get the station constructed."*

After completing her training, Whitson assumed various technical duties at Johnson Space Center. One of these jobs involved returning to Russia to work on that country's space program. During this stay in Russia, she learned the technical details of Russian equipment and helped develop a dual-language computer program. This program was designed to help astronauts interpret flight data, whether they spoke Russian or English.

Whitson found all these tasks to be rewarding, but she also felt impatient to receive a mission assignment and prepare for her first journey into space. She knew that her first assignment might be on a space shuttle voyage, but her greatest hope was to receive a posting to the International Space Station (ISS). The ISS is an internationally funded space research facility that orbits 240 miles above the earth. Construction of the ISS began in 1998, and by October 2000 construction of the facility had reached the point that two- and three-person teams of astronauts were able to live on board for months at a time. An assignment to the ISS would give Whitson an opportunity to perform the kind of long-term experiments she had been planning throughout her career.

In 1999, Whitson received the news she had been waiting a lifetime to hear: she had been assigned to the Expedition Five crew of the International Space Station. Although NASA usually requires astronauts to have at least one short-term spaceflight—such as a shuttle mission—before going on a longer one, the agency waived the requirement in Whitson's case. NASA determined that her ten years of experience with the agency, combined with her successful astronaut training, proved her suitability for the assignment. Not surprisingly, Whitson was tremendously excited at the prospect of living on the ISS. "I don't think I would have turned down anything, but my first choice was to fly on station. I want to get up there, start doing science, and help get the station constructed," she declared.

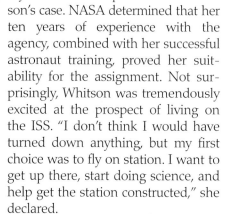

"To say that my first sight of the Earth from orbit was breathtaking or magnificent still seems such a paltry way to describe what I saw and felt," Whitson said. "I would have likened the feeling to having someone turn on the lights after having lived in semi-darkness for years."

Setting Records on the International Space Station

Whitson spent the next two years preparing for her mission. Then, on June 5, 2002, Whitson finally realized her childhood dream when she rode the space shuttle *Endeavour* into orbit. "To say that my first sight of the Earth from orbit was breathtaking or magnificent still seems such a paltry way to describe what I saw and felt," Whitson said. "My first impression was of the clarity of my vision (not even air molecules to get in the way of me seeing what was ahead), [and] it seemed I could see an incredible distance. The next impression was of the richness of the colors that made up our planet and the atmosphere below. The colors were so vibrant that they seemed to have a previously unseen texture. I would liken the feeling to having someone turn on the lights after having lived in semi-darkness for years. I had never really seen anything quite so clearly or with so much color!"

When the space shuttle arrived at the ISS with Whitson and Russian cosmonauts Valeri Korzun and Sergei Treschev, she became the first American

Whitson (right) and Russian cosmonaut Valeri Korzun train underwater in preparation for their mission to the International Space Station.

with a doctorate to join the ISS crew and also the first astronaut without any military service to serve on the station. Because of her scientific expertise, Whitson was officially named the first "science officer" of the ISS. She took great pride in this distinction, but also joked about comparisons to Mr. Spock, the famous alien science officer of the first "Star Trek" television series: "I obviously don't mind the new title, in spite of the fact that

Whitson (center) walks out of crew quarters in the company of other members of the space shuttle Endeavor — *Kenneth Cockrell (front left), Paul Lockhart (front right), Valeri Korzun (middle row left), Sergei Treschev (middle row right), Philippe Perrin (back row left), and Franklin Chang-Diaz (back row right) on the morning of their space flight, June 5, 2002.*

my many supportive friends have sent an incredible amount of "Star Trek"/Mr. Spock-related e-mail," she said. "Live long and prosper."

Once Whitson arrived at the ISS, she spent a lot of time on her research duties. But she also helped with the ongoing construction of the station. For example, she used the station's remote-controlled robot arm system to add new parts to the ISS structure. She also took a four-and-a half-hour spacewalk outside the station on August 16, 2002, so that she could install shielding designed to protect it against tiny "micrometeoroid" strikes. Her spacewalk included a ride at the end of a 45-foot construction crane that cosmonaut Korzun swung from one module to another. Whitson's spacewalk made her the first woman to perform an extravehicular activity (EVA) on the ISS. She later called the experience the highlight of her entire trip. "The experience of flying during the EVA was more like the one you have in your dreams when you fly from place to place without the aid of any craft, only the view from space was much better than anything I had ever dreamed of," she noted. "I definitely felt as though I had wings!"

Creating a Routine in Outer Space

Whitson admitted that it took her a while to get used to some aspects of life on the International Space Station. Adjusting to the station's zero-gravity environment, for example, was a major challenge. According to Whitson, the most difficult aspect of this existence was "adjusting to the fact that my body feels the same in any orientation, but that my head is still trying to put a direction (up/down/ left/right) on things when it doesn't apply."

As one of only three crew members, Whitson also was responsible for performing regular maintenance on the

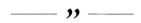

"The experience of flying during the EVA was more like the one you have in your dreams when you fly from place to place without the aid of any craft, only the view from space was much better than anything I had ever dreamed of," Whitson noted. "I definitely felt as though I had wings!"

station's equipment. These duties included monitoring and repairing computer systems, taking inventory of supplies, removing payloads from visiting shuttles, working with the robotic arm, and reviewing messages and plans from mission control. She also had to fit in a one- to two-hour physical workout everyday to keep her bones and muscles strong in the zero gravity environment. Despite all this, Whitson managed to find time for one other special duty during her stay: making the ceremonial first pitch for the 2002 World Series between the Anaheim Angels and San Francisco Giants. She did this by tossing a baseball to one of her ISS colleagues. The toss was videotaped and beamed down to Earth for broadcast before the game on the stadium's giant scoreboard. It was also shown on national television just before the teams took the field to start the game.

Whitson's most rewarding hours on the ISS, however, were spent in her capacity as science officer. During her six months in space, Whitson oversaw 25 experiments in physics, biology, and medicine, including a successful trial growing soybeans in zero gravity. Whitson also supervised an investigation into the process of kidney stone formation in astronauts stationed in outer space. Kidney stones (also called renal stones) are crystals that form in the human body, usually in the kidney, bladder, or urinary tract. The crystals usually form when excess quantities of the minerals calcium and phosphate accumulate in urine. When kidney stones travel into the body's urinary system, they can cause extreme pain and require surgery — thus endangering astronauts and their missions. Whitson's research had previously shown that astronauts are at greater risk of forming kidney stones because their bones lose minerals in zero gravity. Her research efforts on the ISS marked another step forward in NASA's attempts to address this serious issue.

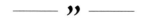

"As we were flying away, I looked back at the station," Whitson recalled. *"It was incredible to see the difference in the structure and say, 'I helped to build that.'"*

Whitson believes that her scientific experiments on the ISS were her most meaningful tasks. "I think one of the most important goals of the station is to figure out how to live in space longer and reduce the risk to the crew members while they're doing it," she explained. Whitson was so devoted to her role as science officer that she often worked on experiments during her off-duty hours. "Being here, living here, is something that I will probably spend the rest of my life striving to find just the right words to try and encompass and convey just a fraction of what makes our endeavors in space so special and essential," she declared.

Returning to Earth's Surface — and Going Below It

After weeks of delays caused by shuttle troubles and bad weather, Whitson finally left the ISS on December 2, 2002. "As we were flying away, I looked back at the station," she recalled. "It was incredible to see the difference in the structure and say, 'I helped to build that.'" On December 7 she returned to Earth with the shuttle *Endeavour,* 184 days and 22 hours after she had left. Her months in zero gravity meant she needed weeks of physical therapy to help rehabilitate her weakened muscles and bones. Nevertheless, the astronaut had no regrets or disappointments regarding

Whitson works
in one of the
laboratories on
the International
Space Station.

The NASA logo for the
space shuttle mission in
which Whitson took part.

Whitson floats along in the zero gravity environment of the
International Space Station.

her time in orbit. "I had wanted to be an astronaut for a very long time," she said. "I had huge expectations. Every one of them has been surpassed."

Just two months after Whitson returned from the ISS, the space shuttle *Columbia* disintegrated after entering the earth's atmosphere on February 1, 2003. All seven people aboard were killed. There are fewer than 150 astronauts in NASA's program, so Whitson knew all of the lost astronauts. In fact, three of the astronauts lost in the explosion were classmates of hers during her NASA training. This tragedy deeply saddened Whitson, but it did not shake her passion for space exploration. "They knew the risks and accepted them," she said of her fallen co-workers.

"Space exploration is part of us as human beings, and I think we have to continue exploration. I'm ready to go back into space as soon as they let me."

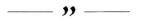

Six months after completing her first space assignment, Whitson entered another hostile environment as commander of an undersea mission for NASA. She was named commander of a four-person team of aquanauts conducting research on the underwater station *Aquarius,* a 45-foot by 9.75-foot capsule that lies 50 feet underwater off the coast of Key Largo, Florida. It is operated by the National Oceanic and Atmospheric Association (NOAA) and the National Undersea Research Center at the University of North Carolina at Wilmington. In June 2003 Whitson and her teammates spent 14 days in the *Aquarius,* which seeks to duplicate conditions that astronauts encounter on space stations. During their stay in the *Aquarius,* Whitson and her crew performed several extravehicular activities (EVAs) — exploratory dives at a nearby coral reef. The aquanauts also collected data on how an enclosed environment affects sleep, hearing, and the body's ability to fight disease, absorb nutrients, and heal wounds. "Arriving into the habitat felt much like our arrival to [the space] station, settling into a new and foreign environment," Whitson noted. "The biggest difference here is that there are certainly a lot more alien life forms floating/swimming around this underwater station than the one circling above the Earth."

Whitson still hopes to return to the International Space Station someday. "My thoughts often travel in the 240-mile orbit [of the ISS] above, wondering about the experiments that they are working on, the sights out the window, the feeling of floating without effort, and [I am] envious of the contentment and satisfaction derived from keeping the station in working order," she stated. "Space exploration is part of us as human beings, and I think we have to continue exploration. I'm ready to go back into space as soon as they let me."

MARRIAGE AND FAMILY

Whitson married Clarence Felton Sams on May 6, 1989. She and her husband, who also works at Johnson Space Center as a research scientist, live in Houston, Texas. They have no children, although Whitson enjoys spending time with her nieces.

HOBBIES AND OTHER INTERESTS

Whitson enjoys such sporting activities as windsurfing, water skiing, weight lifting, basketball, and biking. Another favorite hobby is gardening.

In recognition of her accomplishments, NASA often send Whitson to make presentations at schools around the country. She enjoys these sessions, in which she fields children's many questions about the space program. Whitson also belongs to several professional scientific groups, including the American Association of Biochemistry and Molecular Biology and the New York Academy of Sciences. In addition, she has contributed articles to a variety of scientific journals, including *Biochemistry*, the *Journal of Biological Chemistry*, and the *Journal of Cellular Physiology*.

HONORS AND AWARDS

NASA Exceptional Service Medal: 1995
Randolph Lovelace II Award (American Astronautical Society): 1995
Group Achievement Award (NASA): 1996, for Shuttle-*Mir* Program

FURTHER READING

Periodicals

Current Biography Yearbook, 2003
Des Moines Register, May 21, 2001, p.A1; June 5, 2002, p.A1; Aug. 18, 2002, p. A1; Oct. 15, 2003, p. A1
Houston Chronicle, May 30, 2002, p.A4; Aug. 18, 2002, p.A1; Nov. 10, 2002, p.A1
Ladies Home Journal, Apr. 2003, p.82
Newsday, Feb. 18, 2003, p.A28
Omaha (NE) World-Herald, Apr. 11, 2003, p.A1
Orange County (CA) Register, July 30, 2002, NEWS sec.

Online Articles

http://spaceflight.nasa.gov/station/crew/exp5/intwhitson.html
(*NASA Human Space Flight,* "Preflight Interview: Peggy Whitson," 2002;
"Expedition Five: Letters Home #13," 2002; "Expedition Five: Letters
Home #7, 2002; "Expedition Five: Letters Home #8," 2002)
http://www.uncw.edu/aquarius/2003/06_2003/expd.htm
(*Aquarius: America's Innerspace Station,* "Mission and Project Info:
NEEMO V," 2003; "Journal 7 — Peggy Whitson, Day 4," June 19, 2003)

ADDRESS

Peggy Whitson
Astronaut Office/CB
NASA
Johnson Space Center
Houston, TX 77058

WORLD WIDE WEB SITES

http://www.jsc.nasa.gov
http://www.spaceflight.nasa.gov

Photo and Illustration Credits

Robert Barron/Photos: AP/Wide World Photos; Chris Usher/PEOPLE.

Regina Benjamin/Photos: Copyright © Jeffery Allen Salter/CORBIS. Front cover: John Madere

Jim Cantore/Photos: The Weather Channel.

Marion Donovan/Photos: Marion O'Brien Donovan Papers, Archives Center, National Museum of American History, Smithsonian Institution (pp. 42, 47).

Michael Fay/Photos: Michael Nichols/NGS Image Collection; AP/Wide World Photos (p. 66). Map: NG Maps.

Laura L. Kiessling/Photos: Jeff Miller.

Alvin Poussaint/Photos: Liza Green; courtesy of Harvard Medical School; AP/Wide World Photos (p. 92).

Sandra Steingraber/Photos: Copyright © Jerry Bauer; copyright © Frank DiMeo, Cornell University Photography. Covers: HAVING FAITH (A Berkley Book/Penguin Group) copyright © 2001 by Sandra Steingraber; LIVING DOWNSTREAM (Vintage Books/Random House) copyright © 1997, 1998 by Sandra Steingraber, Ph.D.

Edward Teller/Photos: Nat Farbman/TimeLife Pictures/Getty Images; Lawrence Livermore National Laboratory; copyright © Bettmann/CORBIS; Nat Farbman/TimeLife Pictures/Getty Images; TimeLife Pictures/Getty Images; Ralph Morse/TimeLife Pictures/Getty Images; AP/Wide World Photos; Jacqueline McBride/LLNL.

Peggy Whitson/Photos: NASA; Mikhail Grachyev/Reuters (p. 141).

How to Use the Cumulative Index

Our indexes have a new look. In an effort to make our indexes easier to use, we've combined the Name and General Index into a new, Cumulative Index. This single ready-reference resource covers all the volumes in *Biography Today,* both the general series and the special subject series. The new Cumulative Index contains complete listings of all individuals who have appeared in *Biography Today* since the series began. Their names appear in bold-faced type, followed by the issue in which they appear. The Cumulative Index also includes references for the occupations, nationalities, and ethnic and minority origins of individuals profiled in *Biography Today.*

We have also made some changes to our specialty indexes, the Places of Birth Index and the Birthday Index. To consolidate and to save space, the Places of Birth Index and the Birthday Index will no longer appear in the January and April issues of the softbound subscription series. But these indexes can still be found in the September issue of the softbound subscription series, in the hardbound Annual Cumulation at the end of each year, and in each volume of the special subject series.

General Series

The General Series of *Biography Today* is denoted in the index with the month and year of the issue in which the individual appeared. Each individual also appears in the Annual Cumulation for that year.

Special Subject Series

The Special Subject Series of *Biography Today* are each denoted in the index with an abbreviated form of the series name, plus the number of the volume in which the individual appears. They are listed as follows.

Adams, Ansel .... Artist V.1	(Artists)
Card, Orson Scott .... Author V.14	(Authors)
Diaz, Cameron .... PerfArt V.3	(Performing Artists)
Fay, Michael .... Science V.9	(Scientists & Inventors)
Milbrett, Tiffany .... Sport V.10	(Sports)
Peterson, Roger Tory .... WorLdr V.1	(World Leaders: Environmental Leaders)
Sadat, Anwar .... WorLdr V.2	(World Leaders: Modern African Leaders)
Wolf, Hazel. .... WorLdr V.3	(World Leaders: Environmental Leaders 2)

Updates

Updated information on selected individuals appears in the Appendix at the end of some issues of the *Biography Today* Annual Cumulation. In the index, the original entry is listed first, followed by any updates.

Arafat, Yasir .... Sep 94; Update 94;
Update 95; Update 96; Update 97; Update 98;
Update 00; Update 01; Update 02

Gates, Bill .... Apr 93; Update 98;
Update 00; Science V.5; Update 01

Griffith Joyner, Florence. .... Sport V.1;
Update 98

Sanders, Barry .... Sep 95; Update 99

Spock, Dr. Benjamin .... Sep 95; Update 98

Yeltsin, Boris .... Apr 92; Update 93;
Update 95; Update 96; Update 98; Update 00

Cumulative Index

This cumulative index includes names, occupations, nationalities, and ethnic and minority origins that pertain to all individuals profiled in *Biography Today* since the debut of the series in 1992.

Places of Birth Index

The following index lists the places of birth for the individuals profiled in *Biography Today*. Places of birth are entered under state, province, and/or country.

Birthday Index

October (continued) — Year

28 Gates, Bill 1955
   Roberts, Julia 1967
   Romero, John 1967
   Salk, Jonas 1914
29 Flowers, Vonetta 1973
   Ryder, Winona 1971
31 Candy, John 1950
   Jackson, Peter 1961
   Paterson, Katherine 1932
   Patterson, Ryan 1983
   Pauley, Jane 1950
   Tucker, Chris 1973

November — Year

2 lang, k.d. 1961
   Nelly 1974
3 Arnold, Roseanne 1952
   Ho, David 1952
   Kiraly, Karch 1960
4 Bush, Laura 1946
   Combs, Sean (Puff Daddy) 1969
   Handler, Ruth 1916
7 Bahrke, Shannon 1980
   Canady, Alexa 1950
8 Mittermeier, Russell A. 1949
9 Denton, Sandi
   Sagan, Carl 1934
10 Bates, Daisy . . . . ?1914
11 Blige, Mary J. 1971
   DiCaprio, Leonardo 1974
   Vonnegut, Kurt 1922
12 Andrews, Ned 1980
   Blackmun, Harry 1908
   Harding, Tonya 1970
   Sosa, Sammy 1968
13 Goldberg, Whoopi 1949
14 Boutros-Ghali, Boutros 1922
   Hussein, King 1935
   Lindgren, Astrid 1907
   Rice, Condoleezza 1954
15 O'Keeffe, Georgia 1887
   Pinkwater, Daniel 1941
16 Baiul, Oksana 1977
   Long, Irene D. 1951
   Miyamoto, Shigeru 1952
17 Fuentes, Daisy 1966
   Hanson, Ike 1980
18 Driscoll, Jean 1966
   Felix, Allyson 1985
   Klug, Chris 1972

   Mankiller, Wilma 1945
   Vidal, Christina 1981
19 Collins, Eileen 1956
   Devers, Gail 1966
   Glover, Savion 1973
   Strug, Kerri 1977
21 Aikman, Troy 1966
   Griffey, Ken, Jr. 1969
   Schwikert, Tasha 1984
   Speare, Elizabeth George 1908
22 Boyle, Ryan 1981
   Carmona, Richard 1949
24 Ndeti, Cosmas 1971
25 Grant, Amy 1960
   Mathis, Clint 1976
   McNabb, Donovan 1976
   Thomas, Lewis 1913
26 Patrick, Ruth 1907
   Pine, Elizabeth Michele 1975
   Schulz, Charles 1922
27 Nye, Bill 1955
   White, Jaleel 1977
29 L'Engle, Madeleine 1918
   Lewis, C. S. 1898
   Tubman, William V. S. 1895
30 Jackson, Bo 1962
   Parks, Gordon 1912

December — Year

1 Delson, Brad 1977
2 Hendrickson, Sue 1949
   Macaulay, David 1946
   Seles, Monica 1973
   Spears, Britney 1981
   Watson, Paul 1950
3 Kim Dae-jung . . . . ?1925
   Filipovic, Zlata 1980
4 Banks, Tyra 1973
5 Muniz, Frankie 1985
6 Risca, Viviana 1982
7 Bird, Larry 1956
   Carter, Aaron 1987
8 Rivera, Diego 1886
9 Hopper, Grace Murray 1906
12 Bialik, Mayim 1975
   Frankenthaler, Helen 1928
   Sinatra, Frank 1915
13 Fedorov, Sergei 1969
   Pierce, Tamora 1954
14 Jackson, Shirley 1916

Biography Today

General Series

For ages 9 and above

"Biography Today will be useful in elementary and middle school libraries and in public library children's collections where there is a need for biographies of current personalities. High schools serving reluctant readers may also want to consider a subscription."
— *Booklist,* American Library Association

"Highly recommended for the young adult audience. Readers will delight in the accessible, energetic, tell-all style; teachers, librarians, and parents will welcome the clever format, intelligent and informative text. It should prove especially useful in motivating 'reluctant' readers or literate nonreaders."
— *MultiCultural Review*

"Written in a friendly, almost chatty tone, the profiles offer quick, objective information. While coverage of current figures makes *Biography Today* a useful reference tool, an appealing format and wide scope make it a fun resource to browse." — *School Library Journal*

"The best source for current information at a level kids can understand."
— Kelly Bryant, School Librarian, Carlton, OR

"Easy for kids to read. We love it! Don't want to be without it."
— Lynn McWhirter, School Librarian, Rockford, IL

Biography Today **General Series** includes a unique combination of current biographical profiles that teachers and librarians — and the readers themselves — tell us are most appealing. The **General Series** is available as a 3-issue subscription; hardcover annual cumulation; or subscription plus cumulation.

Within the **General Series**, your readers will find a variety of sketches about:

- Authors
- Musicians
- Political leaders
- Sports figures
- Movie actresses & actors
- Cartoonists
- Scientists
- Astronauts
- TV personalities
- and the movers & shakers in many other fields!

ONE-YEAR SUBSCRIPTION

- 3 softcover issues, 6" x 9"
- Published in January, April, and September
- 1-year subscription, $60
- 150 pages per issue
- 10 profiles per issue
- Contact sources for additional information
- Cumulative General, Places of Birth, and Birthday Indexes

HARDBOUND ANNUAL CUMULATION

- Sturdy 6" x 9" hardbound volume
- Published in December
- $62 per volume
- 450 pages per volume
- 25-30 profiles — includes all profiles found in softcover issues for that calendar year
- Cumulative General, Places of Birth, and Birthday Indexes
- Special appendix features current updates of previous profiles

SUBSCRIPTION AND CUMULATION COMBINATION

- $99 for 3 softcover issues plus the hardbound volume

1992

Paula Abdul
Andre Agassi
Kirstie Alley
Terry Anderson
Roseanne Arnold
Isaac Asimov
James Baker
Charles Barkley
Larry Bird
Judy Blume
Berke Breathed
Garth Brooks
Barbara Bush
George Bush
Fidel Castro
Bill Clinton
Bill Cosby
Diana, Princess of Wales
Shannen Doherty
Elizabeth Dole
David Duke
Gloria Estefan
Mikhail Gorbachev
Steffi Graf
Wayne Gretzky
Matt Groening
Alex Haley
Hammer
Martin Handford
Stephen Hawking
Hulk Hogan
Saddam Hussein
Lee Iacocca
Bo Jackson
Mae Jemison
Peter Jennings
Steven Jobs
Pope John Paul II
Magic Johnson
Michael Jordon
Jackie Joyner-Kersee
Spike Lee
Mario Lemieux
Madeleine L'Engle
Jay Leno
Yo-Yo Ma
Nelson Mandela
Wynton Marsalis
Thurgood Marshall
Ann Martin
Barbara McClintock
Emily Arnold McCully
Antonia Novello

Sandra Day O'Connor
Rosa Parks
Jane Pauley
H. Ross Perot
Luke Perry
Scottie Pippen
Colin Powell
Jason Priestley
Queen Latifah
Yitzhak Rabin
Sally Ride
Pete Rose
Nolan Ryan
H. Norman
    Schwarzkopf
Jerry Seinfeld
Dr. Seuss
Gloria Steinem
Clarence Thomas
Chris Van Allsburg
Cynthia Voigt
Bill Watterson
Robin Williams
Oprah Winfrey
Kristi Yamaguchi
Boris Yeltsin

1993

Maya Angelou
Arthur Ashe
Avi
Kathleen Battle
Candice Bergen
Boutros Boutros-Ghali
Chris Burke
Dana Carvey
Cesar Chavez
Henry Cisneros
Hillary Rodham Clinton
Jacques Cousteau
Cindy Crawford
Macaulay Culkin
Lois Duncan
Marian Wright Edelman
Cecil Fielder
Bill Gates
Sara Gilbert
Dizzy Gillespie
Al Gore
Cathy Guisewite
Jasmine Guy
Anita Hill
Ice-T
Darci Kistler

k.d. lang
Dan Marino
Rigoberta Menchu
Walter Dean Myers
Martina Navratilova
Phyllis Reynolds Naylor
Rudolf Nureyev
Shaquille O'Neal
Janet Reno
Jerry Rice
Mary Robinson
Winona Ryder
Jerry Spinelli
Denzel Washington
Keenen Ivory Wayans
Dave Winfield

1994

Tim Allen
Marian Anderson
Mario Andretti
Ned Andrews
Yasir Arafat
Bruce Babbitt
Mayim Bialik
Bonnie Blair
Ed Bradley
John Candy
Mary Chapin Carpenter
Benjamin Chavis
Connie Chung
Beverly Cleary
Kurt Cobain
F.W. de Klerk
Rita Dove
Linda Ellerbee
Sergei Fedorov
Zlata Filipovic
Daisy Fuentes
Ruth Bader Ginsburg
Whoopi Goldberg
Tonya Harding
Melissa Joan Hart
Geoff Hooper
Whitney Houston
Dan Jansen
Nancy Kerrigan
Alexi Lalas
Charlotte Lopez
Wilma Mankiller
Shannon Miller
Toni Morrison
Richard Nixon
Greg Norman
Severo Ochoa

River Phoenix
Elizabeth Pine
Jonas Salk
Richard Scarry
Emmitt Smith
Will Smith
Steven Spielberg
Patrick Stewart
R.L. Stine
Lewis Thomas
Barbara Walters
Charlie Ward
Steve Young
Kim Zmeskal

1995

Troy Aikman
Jean-Bertrand Aristide
Oksana Baiul
Halle Berry
Benazir Bhutto
Jonathan Brandis
Warren E. Burger
Ken Burns
Candace Cameron
Jimmy Carter
Agnes de Mille
Placido Domingo
Janet Evans
Patrick Ewing
Newt Gingrich
John Goodman
Amy Grant
Jesse Jackson
James Earl Jones
Julie Krone
David Letterman
Rush Limbaugh
Heather Locklear
Reba McEntire
Joe Montana
Cosmas Ndeti
Hakeem Olajuwon
Ashley Olsen
Mary-Kate Olsen
Jennifer Parkinson
Linus Pauling
Itzhak Perlman
Cokie Roberts
Wilma Rudolph
Salt 'N' Pepa
Barry Sanders
William Shatner
Elizabeth George
    Speare

Dr. Benjamin Spock
Jonathan Taylor
   Thomas
Vicki Van Meter
Heather Whitestone
Pedro Zamora

1996

Aung San Suu Kyi
Boyz II Men
Brandy
Ron Brown
Mariah Carey
Jim Carrey
Larry Champagne III
Christo
Chelsea Clinton
Coolio
Bob Dole
David Duchovny
Debbi Fields
Chris Galeczka
Jerry Garcia
Jennie Garth
Wendy Guey
Tom Hanks
Alison Hargreaves
Sir Edmund Hillary
Judith Jamison
Barbara Jordan
Annie Leibovitz
Carl Lewis
Jim Lovell
Mickey Mantle
Lynn Margulis
Iqbal Masih
Mark Messier
Larisa Oleynik
Christopher Pike
David Robinson
Dennis Rodman
Selena
Monica Seles
Don Shula
Kerri Strug
Tiffani-Amber Thiessen
Dave Thomas
Jaleel White

1997

Madeleine Albright
Marcus Allen
Gillian Anderson
Rachel Blanchard
Zachery Ty Bryan
Adam Ezra Cohen
Claire Danes
Celine Dion
Jean Driscoll
Louis Farrakhan
Ella Fitzgerald
Harrison Ford
Bryant Gumbel
John Johnson
Michael Johnson
Maya Lin
George Lucas
John Madden
Bill Monroe
Alanis Morissette
Sam Morrison
Rosie O'Donnell
Muammar el-Qaddafi
Christopher Reeve
Pete Sampras
Pat Schroeder
Rebecca Sealfon
Tupac Shakur
Tabitha Soren
Herbert Tarvin
Merlin Tuttle
Mara Wilson

1998

Bella Abzug
Kofi Annan
Neve Campbell
Sean Combs (Puff
   Daddy)
Dalai Lama (Tenzin
   Gyatso)
Diana, Princess of Wales
Leonardo DiCaprio
Walter E. Diemer
Ruth Handler
Hanson
Livan Hernandez
Jewel
Jimmy Johnson
Tara Lipinski
Jody-Anne Maxwell
Dominique Moceanu
Alexandra Nechita

Brad Pitt
LeAnn Rimes
Emily Rosa
David Satcher
Betty Shabazz
Kordell Stewart
Shinichi Suzuki
Mother Teresa
Mike Vernon
Reggie White
Kate Winslet

1999

Ben Affleck
Jennifer Aniston
Maurice Ashley
Kobe Bryant
Bessie Delany
Sadie Delany
Sharon Draper
Sarah Michelle Gellar
John Glenn
Savion Glover
Jeff Gordon
David Hampton
Lauryn Hill
King Hussein
Lynn Johnston
Shari Lewis
Oseola McCarty
Mark McGwire
Slobodan Milosevic
Natalie Portman
J. K. Rowling
Frank Sinatra
Gene Siskel
Sammy Sosa
John Stanford
Natalia Toro
Shania Twain
Mitsuko Uchida
Jesse Ventura
Venus Williams

2000

Christina Aguilera
K.A. Applegate
Lance Armstrong
Backstreet Boys
Daisy Bates
Harry Blackmun
George W. Bush
Carson Daly
Ron Dayne
Henry Louis Gates, Jr.
Doris Haddock
   (Granny D)
Jennifer Love Hewitt
Chamique Holdsclaw
Katie Holmes
Charlayne Hunter-Gault
Johanna Johnson
Craig Kielburger
John Lasseter
Peyton Manning
Ricky Martin
John McCain
Walter Payton
Freddie Prinze, Jr.
Viviana Risca
Briana Scurry
George Thampy
CeCe Winans

2001

Jessica Alba
Christiane Amanpour
Drew Barrymore
Jeff Bezos
Destiny's Child
Dale Earnhardt
Carly Fiorina
Aretha Franklin
Cathy Freeman
Tony Hawk
Faith Hill
Kim Dae-jung
Madeleine L'Engle
Mariangela Lisanti
Frankie Muniz
*N Sync
Ellen Ochoa
Jeff Probst
Julia Roberts
Carl T. Rowan
Britney Spears
Chris Tucker
Lloyd D. Ward
Alan Webb
Chris Weinke

2002

Aaliyah
Osama bin Laden
Mary J. Blige
Aubyn Burnside
Aaron Carter
Julz Chavez
Dick Cheney
Hilary Duff
Billy Gilman
Rudolph Giuliani
Brian Griese
Jennifer Lopez
Dave Mirra
Dineh Mohajer
Leanne Nakamura
Daniel Radcliffe
Condoleezza Rice
Marla Runyan
Ruth Simmons
Mattie Stepanek
J.R.R. Tolkien
Barry Watson
Tyrone Willingham
Elijah Wood

2003

Yolanda Adams
Olivia Bennett
Mildred Benson
Alexis Bledel
Barry Bonds
Vincent Brooks
Laura Bush
Amanda Bynes
Kelly Clarkson
Vin Diesel
Eminem
Michele Forman
Vicente Fox
Millard Fuller
Josh Hartnett
Dolores Huerta

Sarah Hughes
Enrique Iglesias
Jeanette Lee
John Lewis
Nicklas Lidstrom
Clint Mathis
Donovan McNabb
Nelly
Andy Roddick
Gwen Stefani
Emma Watson
Meg Whitman
Reese Witherspoon
Yao Ming

2004

Natalie Babbitt
David Beckham
Matel Dawson, Jr.
Lisa Leslie
Linkin Park
Irene D. Long
Mandy Moore
Thich Nhat Hanh
Keanu Reeves
Alexa Vega

Biography Today

For ages 9 and above

Subject Series

Expands and complements the General Series and targets specific subject areas . . .

Our readers asked for it! They wanted more biographies, and the *Biography Today* **Subject Series** is our response to that demand. Now your readers can choose their special areas of interest and go on to read about their favorites in those fields. Priced at just $39 per volume, the following specific volumes are included in the *Biography Today* **Subject Series**:

- **Artists**
- **Authors**
- **Performing Artists**
- **Scientists & Inventors**
- **Sports**
- **World Leaders**
  Environmental Leaders
  Modern African Leaders

AUTHORS

"A useful tool for children's assignment needs." — *School Library Journal*

"The prose is workmanlike: report writers will find enough detail to begin sound investigations, and browsers are likely to find someone of interest." — *School Library Journal*

SCIENTISTS & INVENTORS

"The articles are readable, attractively laid out, and touch on important points that will suit assignment needs. Browsers will note the clear writing and interesting details." — *School Library Journal*

"The book is excellent for demonstrating that scientists are real people with widely diverse backgrounds and personal interests. The biographies are fascinating to read." — *The Science Teacher*

SPORTS

"This series should become a standard resource in libraries that serve intermediate students." — *School Library Journal*

ENVIRONMENTAL LEADERS #1

"A tremendous book that fills a gap in the biographical category of books. This is a great reference book." — *Science Scope*

FEATURES AND FORMAT

- Sturdy 6" x 9" hardbound volumes
- Individual volumes, $39 each
- 200 pages per volume
- 10 profiles per volume — targets individuals within a specific subject area
- Contact sources for additional information
- Cumulative General, Places of Birth, and Birthday Indexes

NOTE: There is *no duplication of entries* between the **General Series** of *Biography Today* and the **Subject Series**.

Artists

VOLUME 1

Ansel Adams
Romare Bearden
Margaret Bourke-White
Alexander Calder
Marc Chagall
Helen Frankenthaler
Jasper Johns
Jacob Lawrence
Henry Moore
Grandma Moses
Louise Nevelson
Georgia O'Keeffe
Gordon Parks
I.M. Pei
Diego Rivera
Norman Rockwell
Andy Warhol
Frank Lloyd Wright

Authors

VOLUME 1

Eric Carle
Alice Childress
Robert Cormier
Roald Dahl
Jim Davis
John Grisham
Virginia Hamilton
James Herriot
S.E. Hinton
M.E. Kerr
Stephen King
Gary Larson
Joan Lowery Nixon
Gary Paulsen
Cynthia Rylant
Mildred D. Taylor
Kurt Vonnegut, Jr.
E.B. White
Paul Zindel

VOLUME 2

James Baldwin
Stan and Jan Berenstain
David Macaulay
Patricia MacLachlan
Scott O'Dell
Jerry Pinkney
Jack Prelutsky

Lynn Reid Banks
Faith Ringgold
J.D. Salinger
Charles Schulz
Maurice Sendak
P.L. Travers
Garth Williams

VOLUME 3

Candy Dawson Boyd
Ray Bradbury
Gwendolyn Brooks
Ralph W. Ellison
Louise Fitzhugh
Jean Craighead George
E.L. Konigsburg
C.S. Lewis
Fredrick L. McKissack
Patricia C. McKissack
Katherine Paterson
Anne Rice
Shel Silverstein
Laura Ingalls Wilder

VOLUME 4

Betsy Byars
Chris Carter
Caroline B. Cooney
Christopher Paul Curtis
Anne Frank
Robert Heinlein
Marguerite Henry
Lois Lowry
Melissa Mathison
Bill Peet
August Wilson

VOLUME 5

Sharon Creech
Michael Crichton
Karen Cushman
Tomie dePaola
Lorraine Hansberry
Karen Hesse
Brian Jacques
Gary Soto
Richard Wright
Laurence Yep

VOLUME 6

Lloyd Alexander
Paula Danziger
Nancy Farmer
Zora Neale Hurston

Shirley Jackson
Angela Johnson
Jon Krakauer
Leo Lionni
Francine Pascal
Louis Sachar
Kevin Williamson

VOLUME 7

William H. Armstrong
Patricia Reilly Giff
Langston Hughes
Stan Lee
Julius Lester
Robert Pinsky
Todd Strasser
Jacqueline Woodson
Patricia C. Wrede
Jane Yolen

VOLUME 8

Amelia Atwater-Rhodes
Barbara Cooney
Paul Laurence Dunbar
Ursula K. Le Guin
Farley Mowat
Naomi Shihab Nye
Daniel Pinkwater
Beatrix Potter
Ann Rinaldi

VOLUME 9

Robb Armstrong
Cherie Bennett
Bruce Coville
Rosa Guy
Harper Lee
Irene Gut Opdyke
Philip Pullman
Jon Scieszka
Amy Tan
Joss Whedon

VOLUME 10

David Almond
Joan Bauer
Kate DiCamillo
Jack Gantos
Aaron McGruder
Richard Peck
Andrea Davis Pinkney
Louise Rennison
David Small
Katie Tarbox

VOLUME 11

Laurie Halse Anderson
Bryan Collier
Margaret Peterson
  Haddix
Milton Meltzer
William Sleator
Sonya Sones
Genndy Tartakovsky
Wendelin Van Draanen
Ruth White

VOLUME 12

An Na
Claude Brown
Meg Cabot
Virginia Hamilton
Chuck Jones
Robert Lipsyte
Lillian Morrison
Linda Sue Park
Pam Muñoz Ryan
Lemony Snicket
  (Daniel Handler)

VOLUME 13

Andrew Clements
Eoin Colfer
Sharon Flake
Edward Gorey
Francisco Jiménez
Astrid Lindgren
Chris Lynch
Marilyn Nelson
Tamora Pierce
Virginia Euwer Wolff

VOLUME 14

Orson Scott Card
Russell Freedman
Mary GrandPré
Dan Greenburg
Nikki Grimes
Laura Hillenbrand
Stephen Hillenburg
Norton Juster
Lurlene McDaniel
Stephanie S. Tolan

Performing Artists

VOLUME 1
Jackie Chan
Dixie Chicks
Kirsten Dunst
Suzanne Farrell
Bernie Mac
Shakira
Isaac Stern
Julie Taymor
Usher
Christina Vidal

VOLUME 2
Ashanti
Tyra Banks
Peter Jackson
Norah Jones
Quincy Jones
Avril Lavigne
George López
Marcel Marceau
Eddie Murphy
Julia Stiles

VOLUME 3
Michelle Branch
Cameron Diaz
Missy Elliott
Evelyn Glennie
Benji Madden
Joel Madden
Mike Myers
Fred Rogers
Twyla Tharp
Tom Welling
Yuen Wo-Ping

Scientists & Inventors

VOLUME 1
John Bardeen
Sylvia Earle
Dian Fossey
Jane Goodall
Bernadine Healy
Jack Horner
Mathilde Krim
Edwin Land
Louise & Mary Leakey
Rita Levi-Montalcini
J. Robert Oppenheimer
Albert Sabin
Carl Sagan
James D. Watson

VOLUME 2
Jane Brody
Seymour Cray
Paul Erdös
Walter Gilbert
Stephen Jay Gould
Shirley Ann Jackson
Raymond Kurzweil
Shannon Lucid
Margaret Mead
Garrett Morgan
Bill Nye
Eloy Rodriguez
An Wang

VOLUME 3
Luis W. Alvarez
Hans A. Bethe
Gro Harlem Brundtland
Mary S. Calderone
Ioana Dumitriu
Temple Grandin
John Langston
  Gwaltney
Bernard Harris
Jerome Lemelson
Susan Love
Ruth Patrick
Oliver Sacks
Richie Stachowski

VOLUME 4
David Attenborough
Robert Ballard
Ben Carson

Eileen Collins
Biruté Galdikas
Lonnie Johnson
Meg Lowman
Forrest Mars Sr.
Akio Morita
Janese Swanson

VOLUME 5
Steve Case
Douglas Engelbart
Shawn Fanning
Sarah Flannery
Bill Gates
Laura Groppe
Grace Murray Hopper
Steven Jobs
Rand and Robyn Miller
Shigeru Miyamoto
Steve Wozniak

VOLUME 6
Hazel Barton
Alexa Canady
Arthur Caplan
Francis Collins
Gertrude Elion
Henry Heimlich
David Ho
Kenneth Kamler
Lucy Spelman
Lydia Villa-Komaroff

VOLUME 7
Tim Berners-Lee
France Córdova
Anthony S. Fauci
Sue Hendrickson
Steve Irwin
John Forbes Nash, Jr.
Jerri Nielsen
Ryan Patterson
Nina Vasan
Gloria WilderBrathwaite

VOLUME 8
Deborah Blum
Richard Carmona
Helene Gayle
Dave Kapell
Adriana C. Ocampo
John Romero
Jamie Rubin
Jill Tarter
Earl Warrick
Edward O. Wilson

VOLUME 9
Robert Barron
Regina Benjamin
Jim Cantore
Marion Donovan
Michael Fay
Laura L. Kiessling
Alvin Poussaint
Sandra Steingraber
Edward Teller
Peggy Whitson

Sports

VOLUME 1
Hank Aaron
Kareem Abdul-Jabbar
Hassiba Boulmerka
Susan Butcher
Beth Daniel
Chris Evert
Ken Griffey, Jr.
Florence Griffith Joyner
Grant Hill
Greg LeMond
Pelé
Uta Pippig
Cal Ripken, Jr.
Arantxa Sanchez
  Vicario
Deion Sanders
Tiger Woods

VOLUME 2
Muhammad Ali
Donovan Bailey
Gail Devers
John Elway
Brett Favre
Mia Hamm
Anfernee "Penny"
  Hardaway
Martina Hingis
Gordie Howe
Jack Nicklaus
Richard Petty
Dot Richardson
Sheryl Swoopes
Steve Yzerman

221

VOLUME 3

Joe Dumars
Jim Harbaugh
Dominik Hasek
Michelle Kwan
Rebecca Lobo
Greg Maddux
Fatuma Roba
Jackie Robinson
John Stockton
Picabo Street
Pat Summitt
Amy Van Dyken

VOLUME 4

Wilt Chamberlain
Brandi Chastain
Derek Jeter
Karch Kiraly
Alex Lowe
Randy Moss
Se Ri Pak
Dawn Riley
Karen Smyers
Kurt Warner
Serena Williams

VOLUME 5

Vince Carter
Lindsay Davenport
Lisa Fernandez
Fu Mingxia
Jaromir Jagr
Marion Jones
Pedro Martinez
Warren Sapp
Jenny Thompson
Karrie Webb

VOLUME 6

Jennifer Capriati
Stacy Dragila
Kevin Garnett
Eddie George
Alex Rodriguez
Joe Sakic
Annika Sorenstam
Jackie Stiles
Tiger Woods
Aliy Zirkle

VOLUME 7

Tom Brady
Tara Dakides
Alison Dunlap
Sergio Garcia
Allen Iverson
Shirley Muldowney
Ty Murray
Patrick Roy
Tasha Schwiker

VOLUME 8

Simon Ammann
Shannon Bahrke
Kelly Clark
Vonetta Flowers
Cammi Granato
Chris Klug
Jonny Moseley
Apolo Ohno
Sylke Otto
Ryne Sanborn
Jim Shea, Jr.

VOLUME 9

Tori Allen
Layne Beachley
Sue Bird
Fabiola da Silva
Randy Johnson
Jason Kidd
Tony Stewart
Michael Vick
Ted Williams
Jay Yelas

VOLUME 10

Ryan Boyle
Natalie Coughlin
Allyson Felix
Dallas Friday
Jean-Sébastien Giguère
Phil Jackson
Keyshawn Johnson
Tiffeny Milbrett
Alfonso Soriano
Diana Taurasi

World Leaders

VOLUME 1: Environmental Leaders 1

Edward Abbey
Renee Askins
David Brower
Rachel Carson
Marjory Stoneman
  Douglas
Dave Foreman
Lois Gibbs
Wangari Maathai
Chico Mendes
Russell A. Mittermeier
Margaret and Olaus J.
  Murie
Patsy Ruth Oliver
Roger Tory Peterson
Ken Saro-Wiwa
Paul Watson
Adam Werbach

VOLUME 2: Modern African Leaders

Mohammed Farah
  Aidid
Idi Amin
Hastings Kamuzu Banda
Haile Selassie
Hassan II
Kenneth Kaunda
Jomo Kenyatta
Winnie Mandela
Mobutu Sese Seko
Robert Mugabe
Kwame Nkrumah
Julius Kambarage
  Nyerere
Anwar Sadat
Jonas Savimbi
Léopold Sédar Senghor
William V. S. Tubman

VOLUME 3: Environmental Leaders 2

John Cronin
Dai Qing
Ka Hsaw Wa
Winona LaDuke
Aldo Leopold
Bernard Martin
Cynthia Moss
John Muir
Gaylord Nelson
Douglas Tompkins
Hazel Wolf